Learning Shiny

Make the most of R's dynamic capabilities
and create web applications with Shiny

Hernán G. Resnizky

[PACKT] open source ✳
PUBLISHING   community experience distilled

BIRMINGHAM - MUMBAI

Learning Shiny

First published: October 2015

Production reference: 1141015

Published by Packt Publishing Ltd.
Livery Place
35 Livery Street
Birmingham B3 2PB, UK.

ISBN 978-1-78528-090-0

www.packtpub.com

Credits

Author
Hernán G. Resnizky

Reviewers
Dean Attali

William Kyle Hamilton

Achyutuni Sri Krishna Rao

Commissioning Editor
Kunal Parikh

Acquisition Editors
Shaon Basu

Larissa Pinto

Content Development Editor
Ritika Singh

Technical Editor
Shiny Poojary

Copy Editor
Kausambhi Majumdar

Project Coordinator
Judie Jose

Proofreader
Safis Editing

Indexer
Rekha Nair

Graphics
Disha Haria

Production Coordinator
Melwyn D'sa

Cover Work
Melwyn D'sa

About the Author

Hernán G. Resnizky is a data scientist who is actually working as a freelance consultant in Argentina. He has worked for national and international clients from diverse industries in different domains related to data handling and analysis, such as data visualization, text mining, machine learning modeling, and so on. For over two years, he worked as a senior data scientist for Despegar (http://www.despegar.com/), the leading online travel agency in Latin America.

Regarding his academic background, Hernán has completed a licentiate degree (a five-year study program that is equivalent to a bachelor's and a master's degree) in sociology from the University of Buenos Aires. Also, he has completed his masters of science courses in data mining from the same university.

Hernán has a blog, www.hernanresnizky.com, where he writes about data science and R-related topics. Also, he has reviewed *Web Application Development with R Using Shiny* for Packt Publishing in the past.

Acknowledgements

I think it would be totally unfair if I didn't start this acknowledgement by thanking the whole R community, as I believe that a considerable part of my knowledge of R and Shiny was gained from gathering information from forums, blogs, and tutorials. In this sense, if I had to think of someone in particular, I should thank Hadley Wickham not only for his packages, but also for his wonderful tutorials, and from RStudio's Shiny crew, I would like to thank Joe Cheng and Winston Chang for their constant efforts to make the Shiny project grow by answering questions, posting articles, and even sharing their repositories.

I would also like to dedicate this book to my former colleagues at Despegar (http://www.despegar.com/) where I spent over two years of constant learning facing new challenges every day, to my clients who believe in my capabilities every day, and to my former classmates and professors at the University of Buenos Aires.

Of course, I can't leave out my family and friends, who despite not understanding completely what I do for a living, always encouraged me to carry on. Finally, I would like to thank my girlfriend for supporting me in this enriching but tough process of writing a book.

About the Reviewers

Dean Attali is a software engineer, technical consultant, and freelance technical writer. He studied computer science at the University of Waterloo, Canada, and has years of experience working for large companies (Google and IBM) as well as small startups (`tagged.com`, `wish.com`, and, `glittr.com`). After spending a few years in San Francisco and getting a good taste of the Silicon Valley tech life, Dean was curious to see what academia had to offer and went on to pursue a master's degree from the University of British Columbia in Vancouver, Canada.

Dean was introduced to R while he was in graduate school, and he quickly developed a passion for R and open source, with a special interest in the Shiny framework. He is now an active member of the R community and is the author of several R packages, most notably "shinyjs".

Apart from coding, Dean is also addicted to playing soccer, travelling at any given (and nongiven) moment, getting into philosophical debates, and meeting new people. You can learn more, or just say "hello", by visiting him at `http://deanattali.com`.

William Kyle Hamilton earned his bachelor of arts degree in psychology with a minor in political science from the University of California, Merced in 2012 and is now a PhD student in the Health Psychology program at the University of California, Merced. In addition to this, William runs workshops for academic requesters who wish to use Amazon Mechanical Turk for their studies. William is a community member of the rOpenSci group and has authored the R packages: IRTShiny, MAVIS, RCryptsy, and RStars. Additionally, William serves as a board member for the UC Merced Alumni Association, as well for the Merced County Advisory Board on Alcohol and Drug Problems.

Achyutuni Sri Krishna Rao is an R programmer, data scientist, and civil engineer with more than 4 years of work experience in the public sector and corporate companies. Currently, he is a data scientist associate consultant in one of the leading pharmaceutical consultant firms. He loves to work in the domain of healthcare, power, and construction industry. He strongly believes in the application of Big Data-driven solutions in sectors heavily dominated by core engineering principles.

With a master's in Enterprise Business Analytics from NUS, Achyutuni is a freelancer and R code blogger too. He blogs about providing holistic analytical solutions on open source data using a multitude of machine learning algorithms in R. He is also a corporate trainer in R programming.

www.PacktPub.com

Support files, eBooks, discount offers, and more

For support files and downloads related to your book, please visit www.PacktPub.com.

Did you know that Packt offers eBook versions of every book published, with PDF and ePub files available? You can upgrade to the eBook version at www.PacktPub.com and as a print book customer, you are entitled to a discount on the eBook copy. Get in touch with us at service@packtpub.com for more details.

At www.PacktPub.com, you can also read a collection of free technical articles, sign up for a range of free newsletters and receive exclusive discounts and offers on Packt books and eBooks.

https://www2.packtpub.com/books/subscription/packtlib

Do you need instant solutions to your IT questions? PacktLib is Packt's online digital book library. Here, you can search, access, and read Packt's entire library of books.

Why subscribe?

- Fully searchable across every book published by Packt
- Copy and paste, print, and bookmark content
- On demand and accessible via a web browser

Free access for Packt account holders

If you have an account with Packt at www.PacktPub.com, you can use this to access PacktLib today and view 9 entirely free books. Simply use your login credentials for immediate access.

Table of Contents

Preface

R is a growing language that is gaining more and more space among data scientists. With over 7,000 packages, you can cover every stage within R: from data extraction, cleansing, and processing to advanced analysis, modelling, or visualization. In this context, Shiny is the tool that will take your R code to the next level, as you will be able to share all your outcomes with anyone through a dynamic web application. Shiny is not just a dashboard tool, but it is the gateway to unveiling hidden facts about data, even for nonexpert users. In other words, developing a Shiny application is like providing access to the R universe.

What this book covers

Chapter 1, Introducing R, RStudio, and Shiny, is a brief introduction to R, RStudio, and Shiny, and it contains the necessary information to install them.

Chapter 2, First Steps towards Programming in R, is a general introduction to some key concepts and basic operations in R.

Chapter 3, An Introduction to Data Processing in R, covers some techniques to clean and process data in R using the functions of specific packages. Data processing is definitely one of the key aspects to take into account in order to produce a successful application.

Chapter 4, Shiny Structure – Reactivity Concepts, introduces the reader to Shiny's internal structure and logic.

Chapter 5, Shiny in Depth – A Deep Dive into Shiny's World, examines the different possibilities within the Shiny structure for each of its components. For the user interface section, it presents the different elements available, and for the backend section, it gives some hints about how to optimally organize code.

Chapter 6, Using R's Visualization Alternatives in Shiny, covers the most important graphical packages in R and how to include their outcomes in a Shiny application. This is a key aspect when developing an application, as graphics are usually one of the most common ways to present information in a web application.

Chapter 7, Advanced Functions in Shiny, introduces some advanced functions to control more complex interactions and explains how to use them.

Chapter 8, Shiny and HTML/JavaScript, explains how to include custom JavaScript, HTML, and CSS code in a Shiny application, as Shiny's frontend is HTML-based/ JavaScript-based.

Chapter 9, Interactive Graphics in Shiny, covers two topics, whose common root is interaction with graphics. Firstly, the newly released functionality of Shiny's event listener within R's standard graphics and then the generation of custom JavaScript visualizations, and how to include them in a Shiny application.

Chapter 10, Sharing Applications, introduces different possibilities to publish applications right from passing the entire code to uploading it to a server and making it accessible via URL.

Chapter 11, From White Paper to a Full Application, simulates a real-world situation where a web application is needed and explains the whole process from scratch in a holistic way. It not only explains the code, but also gives some tips about how to structure it and how to communicate with data.

What you need for this book

The software used in this book is free and open source and is available for Linux, Mac, and Windows. An internet connection is necessary for some of the topics covered in this book.

Who this book is for

This book is suitable even for readers with no experience in R, Shiny, or HTML at all. However, having some previous knowledge in any of these fields will definitely be an advantage to understand this book quickly.

Conventions

In this book, you will find a number of text styles that distinguish between different kinds of information. Here are some examples of these styles and an explanation of their meaning.

Code words in text, database table names, folder names, filenames, file extensions, pathnames, dummy URLs, user input, and Twitter handles are shown as follows: "If it is a `.rda` or `.RData` file, it will open in both."

A block of code is set as follows:

```
#Load XML library
library(XML)

#URL Public API Worldbank Data Catalog in XML format
url <- "http://api.worldbank.org/v2/datacatalog?format=xml"

#Load XML document
xml.obj <- xmlTreeParse(url)
```

Any command-line input or output is written as follows:

```
> class(xml.obj)

[1] "XMLDocument"        "XMLAbstractDocument"
```

New terms and **important words** are shown in bold. Words that you see on the screen, for example, in menus or dialog boxes, appear in the text like this: "In RStudio, whenever a function is declared, it will appear in the **Environment** section under the **Functions** section:"

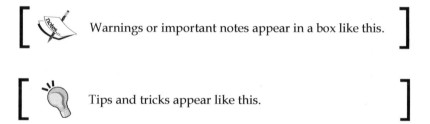

Warnings or important notes appear in a box like this.

Tips and tricks appear like this.

Reader feedback

Feedback from our readers is always welcome. Let us know what you think about this book—what you liked or disliked. Reader feedback is important for us as it helps us develop titles that you will really get the most out of.

To send us general feedback, simply e-mail feedback@packtpub.com, and mention the book's title in the subject of your message.

If there is a topic that you have expertise in and you are interested in either writing or contributing to a book, see our author guide at www.packtpub.com/authors.

Customer support

Now that you are the proud owner of a Packt book, we have a number of things to help you to get the most from your purchase.

Downloading the example code

You can download the example code files from your account at `http://www.packtpub.com` for all the Packt Publishing books you have purchased. If you purchased this book elsewhere, you can visit `http://www.packtpub.com/support` and register to have the files e-mailed directly to you.

Downloading the color images of this book

We also provide you with a PDF file that has color images of the screenshots/diagrams used in this book. The color images will help you better understand the changes in the output. You can download this file from: `https://www.packtpub.com/sites/default/files/downloads/0900OS_ColoredImages.pdf`.

Errata

Although we have taken every care to ensure the accuracy of our content, mistakes do happen. If you find a mistake in one of our books—maybe a mistake in the text or the code—we would be grateful if you could report this to us. By doing so, you can save other readers from frustration and help us improve subsequent versions of this book. If you find any errata, please report them by visiting `http://www.packtpub.com/submit-errata`, selecting your book, clicking on the **Errata Submission Form** link, and entering the details of your errata. Once your errata are verified, your submission will be accepted and the errata will be uploaded to our website or added to any list of existing errata under the Errata section of that title.

To view the previously submitted errata, go to `https://www.packtpub.com/books/content/support` and enter the name of the book in the search field. The required information will appear under the **Errata** section.

Piracy

Piracy of copyrighted material on the Internet is an ongoing problem across all media. At Packt, we take the protection of our copyright and licenses very seriously. If you come across any illegal copies of our works in any form on the Internet, please provide us with the location address or website name immediately so that we can pursue a remedy.

Please contact us at copyright@packtpub.com with a link to the suspected pirated material.

We appreciate your help in protecting our authors and our ability to bring you valuable content.

Questions

If you have a problem with any aspect of this book, you can contact us at questions@packtpub.com, and we will do our best to address the problem.

1

Introducing R, RStudio, and Shiny

In this chapter, the main objective will be to learn how to install all the needed components to build an application in R with Shiny. Additionally, some general ideas about what R is will be covered in order to be able to dive deeper into programming using R.

The following topics will be covered in this chapter:

- A brief introduction to R, RStudio, and Shiny
- Installation of R and Shiny
- General tips and tricks

About R

As stated on the R-project main website:

> *"R is a language and environment for statistical computing and graphics."*

R is a successor of S and is a GNU project. This means, briefly, that anyone can have access to its source codes and can modify or adapt it to their needs. Nowadays, it is gaining territory over classic commercial software, and it is, along with Python, the most used language for statistics and data science.

Regarding R's main characteristics, the following can be considered:

- **Object oriented**: R is a language that is composed mainly of objects and functions. *Chapter 2, First Steps towards Programming in R*, and *Chapter 3, An Introduction to Data Processing in R*, will cover object and function handling in R.

- **Can be easily contributed to**: Similar to GNU projects, R is constantly being enriched by users' contributions either by making their codes accessible via "packages" or libraries, or by editing/improving its source code. There are actually almost 7000 packages in the common R repository, **Comprehensive R Archive Network (CRAN)**. Additionally, there are other R repositories of public access, such as the bioconductor project which contains packages for bioinformatics.

- **Runtime execution**: Unlike C or Java, R does not need compilation. This means that you can, for instance, write 2 + 2 in the console and it will return the value.

- **Extensibility**: The R functionalities can be extended through the installation of packages and libraries. Standard proven libraries can be found in CRAN repositories and are accessible directly from R by typing `install.packages()`.

Installing R

R can be installed in every operating system. It is highly recommended to download the program directly from `http://cran.rstudio.com/` when working on Windows or Mac OS. On Ubuntu, R can be easily installed from the terminal as follows:

```
sudo apt-get update
sudo apt-get install r-base
sudo apt-get install r-base-dev
```

The installation of `r-base-dev` is highly recommended as it is a package that enables users to compile the R packages from source, that is, maintain the packages or install additional R packages directly from the R console using the `install.packages()` command.

To install R on other UNIX-based operating systems, visit the following links:

- `http://cran.rstudio.com/`
- `http://cran.r-project.org/doc/manuals/r-release/R-admin.html#Obtaining-R`

A quick guide to R

When working on Windows, R can be launched via its application. After the installation, it is available as any other program on Windows. When opening the program, a window like this will appear:

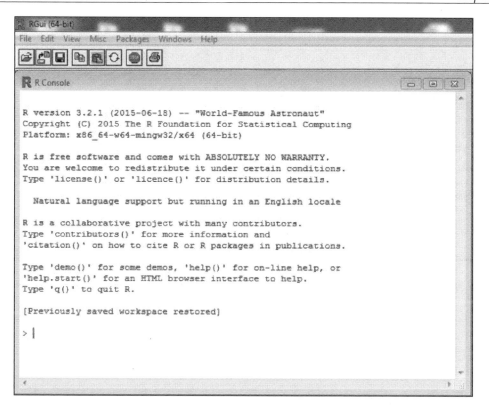

When working on Linux, you can access the R console directly by typing R on the command line:

In both the cases, R executes in runtime. This means that you can type in code, press *Enter*, and the result will be given immediately as follows:

```
> 2+2
[1] 4
```

The R application in any operating system does not provide an easy environment to develop code. For this reason, it is highly recommended (not only to write web applications in R with Shiny, but for any task you want to perform in R) to use an **Integrated Development Environment (IDE)**.

The topics related to the R language are covered mainly in *Chapter 2, First Steps towards Programming in R*, and *Chapter 3, An Introduction to Data Processing in R*.

About RStudio

As with other programming languages, there is a huge variety of IDEs available for R. IDEs are applications that make code development easier and clearer for the programmer. RStudio is one of the most important ones for R, and it is especially recommended to write web applications in R with Shiny because this contains features specially designed for this purpose. Additionally, RStudio provides facilities to write C++, Latex, or HTML documents and also integrates them to the R code.

RStudio also provides version control, project management, and debugging features among many others.

Installing RStudio

RStudio for desktop computers can be downloaded from its official website at http://www.rstudio.com/products/rstudio/download/ where you can get versions of the software for Windows, MAC OS X, Ubuntu, Debian, and Fedora.

A quick guide to RStudio

Before installing and running RStudio, it is important to have R installed. As it is an IDE and not the programming language, it will not work at all. The following screenshot shows RStudio's starting view:

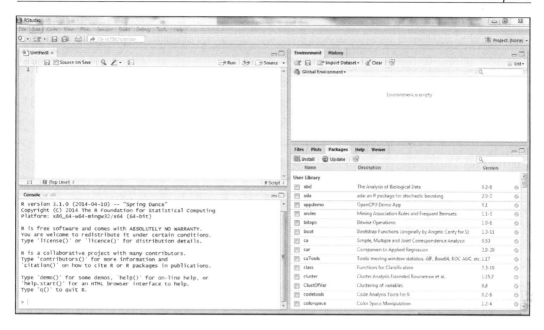

At the first glance, the following four main windows are available:

- **Text editor**: This provides facilities to write R scripts such as highlighting and a code completer (when hitting *Tab*, you can see the available options to complete the code written). It is also possible to include R code in an HTML, Latex, or C++ piece of code.

- **Environment and history**: They are defined as follows:

    ○ In the **Environment** section, you can see the active objects in each environment. By clicking on **Global Environment** (which is the environment shown by default), you can change the environment and see the active objects. You can find more information about environments in a chapter dedicated to this topic in the book *Advanced R*, by *Hadley Wickham*. It is available at `http://adv-r.had.co.nz/Environments.html`.

    ○ In the **History** tab, the pieces of codes executed are stored line by line. You can select one or more lines and send them either to the editor or to the console. In addition, you can look up for a certain specific piece of code by typing it in the textbox in the top right part of this window.

- **Console**: This is an exact equivalent of R console, as described in *Quick guide of R*.

- **Tabs**: The different tabs are defined as follows:

    ○ **Files**: This consists of a file browser with several additional features (renaming, deleting, and copying). Clicking on a file will open it in editor or the **Environment** tab depending on the type of the file. If it is a .rda or .RData file, it will open in both. If it is a text file, it will open in one of them.

    ○ **Plots**: Whenever a plot is executed, it will be displayed in that tab.

    ○ **Packages**: This shows a list of available and active packages. When the package is active, it will appear as clicked. Packages can also be installed interactively by clicking on **Install Packages**.

    ○ **Help**: This is a window to seek and read active packages' documentation.

    ○ **Viewer**: This enables us to see the HTML-generated content within RStudio.

Along with numerous features, RStudio also provides keyboard shortcuts. A few of them are listed as follows:

Description	Windows/Linux	OSX
Complete the code.	*Tab*	*Tab*
Run the selected piece of code. If no piece of code is selected, the active line is run.	*Ctrl + Enter*	⌘ *+ Enter*
Comment the selected block of code.	*Ctrl + Shift + C*	⌘ *+ /*
Create a section of code, which can be expanded or compressed by clicking on the arrow to the left. Additionally, it can be accessed by clicking on it in the bottom left menu.	#####	#####
Find and replace.	*Ctrl + F*	⌘ *+ F*

The following screenshots show how a block of code can be collapsed by clicking on the arrow and how it can be accessed quickly by clicking on its name in the bottom-left part of the window:

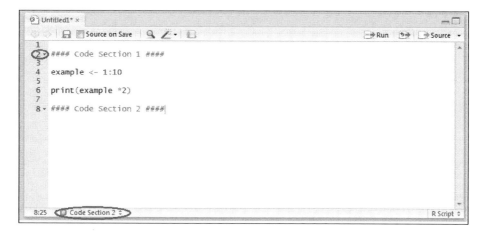

Clicking on the circled arrow will collapse the `Section 1` block, as follows:

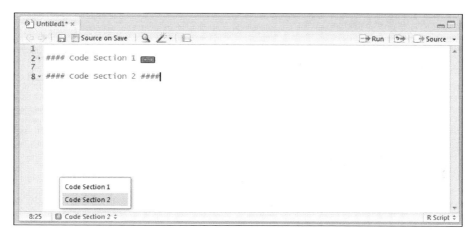

The full list of shortcuts can be found at `https://support.rstudio.com/hc/en-us/articles/200711853-Keyboard-Shortcuts`.

 For further information about other RStudio features, the full documentation is available at `https://support.rstudio.com/hc/en-us/categories/200035113-Documentation`.

About Shiny

Shiny is a package created by RStudio, which enables to easily interface R with a web browser. As stated in its official documentation, *Shiny is a web application framework for R that makes it incredibly easy to build interactive web applications with R.*

One of its main advantages is that there is no need to combine R code with HTML/JavaScript code as the framework already contains prebuilt features that cover the most commonly used functionalities in a web interactive application. There is a wide range of software that has web application functionalities, especially oriented to interactive data visualization. What are the advantages of using R/Shiny then, you ask? They are as follows:

- It is free not only in terms of money but (as with all GNU projects) in terms of freedom. As stated in the GNU main page: *To understand the concept, you should think of "free" as in "free speech", not as in "free beer".* Free software is a matter of the users' freedom to run, copy, distribute, study, change, and improve the software.

- All the possibilities of a powerful language such as R is available. Thanks to its contributive essence, you can develop a web application that can display any R-generated output. This means that you can, for instance, run complex statistical models and return the output in a friendly way in the browser, obtain and integrate data from the various sources and formats (for instance, SQL, XML, JSON, and so on) the way you need, and subset, process, and dynamically aggregate the data the way you want. These options are not available (or are much more difficult to accomplish) under most of the commercial BI tools.

Installing and loading Shiny

As with any other package available in the CRAN repositories, the easiest way to install Shiny is by executing `install.packages("shiny")`.

The following output should appear on the console:

```
> install.packages("shiny")
Installing package into 'C:/               /Documents/R/win-library/3.1'
(as 'lib' is unspecified)
also installing the dependencies 'Rcpp', 'httpuv', 'mime', 'htmltools', 'R6'

trying URL 'http://cran.rstudio.com/bin/windows/contrib/3.1/Rcpp_0.11.3.zip'
Content type 'application/zip' length 3029311 bytes (2.9 Mb)
opened URL
downloaded 2.9 Mb

trying URL 'http://cran.rstudio.com/bin/windows/contrib/3.1/httpuv_1.3.2.zip'
Content type 'application/zip' length 869817 bytes (849 Kb)
opened URL
downloaded 849 Kb

trying URL 'http://cran.rstudio.com/bin/windows/contrib/3.1/mime_0.2.zip'
Content type 'application/zip' length 34989 bytes (34 Kb)
opened URL
downloaded 34 Kb

trying URL 'http://cran.rstudio.com/bin/windows/contrib/3.1/htmltools_0.2.6.zip'
Content type 'application/zip' length 85960 bytes (83 Kb)
opened URL
downloaded 83 Kb

trying URL 'http://cran.rstudio.com/bin/windows/contrib/3.1/R6_2.0.1.zip'
Content type 'application/zip' length 123236 bytes (120 Kb)
opened URL
downloaded 120 Kb

trying URL 'http://cran.rstudio.com/bin/windows/contrib/3.1/shiny_0.10.2.1.zip'
Content type 'application/zip' length 1328853 bytes (1.3 Mb)
opened URL
downloaded 1.3 Mb

package 'Rcpp' successfully unpacked and MD5 sums checked
package 'httpuv' successfully unpacked and MD5 sums checked
package 'mime' successfully unpacked and MD5 sums checked
package 'htmltools' successfully unpacked and MD5 sums checked
package 'R6' successfully unpacked and MD5 sums checked
package 'shiny' successfully unpacked and MD5 sums checked
```

Due to R's extensibility, many of its packages use elements (mostly functions) from other packages. For this reason, these packages are loaded or installed when the package that is dependent on them is loaded or installed. This is called dependency. Shiny (on its 0.10.2.1 version) depends on Rcpp, httpuv, mime, htmltools, and R6.

An R session is started only with the minimal packages loaded. So if functions from other packages are used, they need to be loaded before using them. The corresponding command for this is as follows:

```
library(shiny)
```

When installing a package, the package name must be quoted but when loading the package, it must be unquoted.

Summary

After these instructions, the reader should be able to install all the fundamental elements to create a web application with Shiny. Additionally, he or she should have acquired at least a general idea of what R and the R project is.

The next chapter will focus on the first steps of programming in R and the key elements of this language.

2
First Steps towards Programming in R

This chapter is a general introduction to classes, objects, and functions in R. Now, we now know that R is an object-oriented language. Conceptually, as any other language of its kind, R has three main elements, as follows:

- Classes
- Objects
- Functions

This chapter will cover the following topics:

- **Object-oriented programming** (OOP) concepts in R
- Vectors and arrays
- Lists
- Decision making and looping constructs

Object-oriented programming concepts

As in any other object-oriented programming language, a class in R is an abstract definition of an object type with specific attributes associated to it. For instance, for an eventual `dog` class (which is a general definition of a dog), we could say that it has the `color`, `size`, `age`, and so on attributes.

An object is an instance of a specific class. Continuing with the previous example, we could have a `Dog1` object whose attributes can be the following:

- `color: "brown"`
- `size: 5.5 inch`
- `age: 3 years`

In R, the attributes of an object can be accessed by typing `attr(object, "attribute")`, for instance:

```
data(iris)
attributes(iris)
```

In this example, a data frame object (data frame objects will be explained later in this chapter) called `iris` is loaded, which has the `names`, `row.names`, and `class` attributes (R considers the class of an object an attribute as well). In most cases, many of the values for these attributes in a particular object can be accessed by typing either `attr(object, "attribute")` or the name of the attribute as follows:

```
attr(iris,"names")
names(iris)
```

Normally, the second option will be used.

Finally, functions are usually routines to which a set of values is given (input) and an output is returned. They can be classified in two big groups: the ones that return a value and the ones that don't return a value. For example, `save` and `print` functions, among others. A very easy way to distinguish them is by testing whether the output can be assigned to a variable:

```
> var1 <- sum(c(4,3,2))
> var1
[1]  9


> var1 <- cat(9)
9
> var1
NULL
```

In the first case, the output of the `sum` function is assigned to `var1`. So, when typing the name of the variable, it outputs its value to the console. In the second case, `cat` just outputs the value to the console but cannot assign this output to a variable. For this reason, `var1` is created but no value is assigned to it. So when it is typed, it returns `NULL`, which means that it has no value associated with it.

In the following example, a function that returns a value is declared:

```
test.function <- function(a,b,c){
  result <- (a * b) + c
  return(result)
}
```

In RStudio, whenever a function is declared, it will appear in the **Environment** section under the **Functions** section:

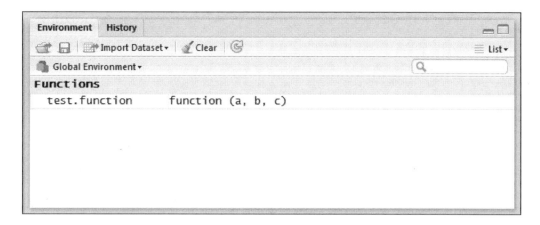

The code of a function can be seen when its name is typed without any parentheses:

```
test.function
## function(a,b,c){
##   result <- (a * b) + c
##   return(result)
## }
```

Once the function is declared, it is ready to be used:

```
> test.function(2,3,1)
```

```
[1] 7
```

Variables in R

Unlike Java or C#, R enables total flexibility in the assignment of variables. This means that you can assign objects of different types to the same variable. This will cause overriding:

```
var1 <- 10
var1 <- "a string"
```

In this case, for instance, R will not throw an error for var1. In addition, there is no need to pre-declare the class of the variable.

The assignment of variables in R can be done in the following three ways:

- `<-` or `->`: These arrows assign the corresponding value to a variable. However, the first alternative is more common:

```
var1 <- 10
10 -> var1
```

- `=`: This is similar to `<-` or `->`.

 As in most programming languages, it is important to keep in mind that whenever a comparison is needed, `==` must be used.

- `assign()`: This is a function with the name of the variable as its first parameter and the value as its second:

```
> assign("var1",6)
```

For conventional variable assignments, there is no need to use this function. However, it becomes particularly useful if dynamic naming of a variable is needed (a function could eventually be used to determine the name of a variable in the first argument of the function) or, if needed, a variable can be assigned to another environment (this issue will not be covered in this book, for further information about this, visit `http://adv-r.had.co.nz/Environments.html`).

R is case sensitive. This means that upper and lower case are relevant. For instance, the `var1` and `Var1` variables are semantically two completely different objects.

Classes in depth

R has the following six fundamental or *atomic* classes:

- **Character**: When assigning a character value to a variable, the corresponding string must be quoted.
- **Numeric**: Decimal numbers.
- **Integer**: Non-decimal numbers.
- **Complex**: Complex numbers.
- **Logical**: `TRUE`/`FALSE` values.
- **Raw**: As explained in the help section of R—the raw type is intended to hold raw bytes. This is very rarely used.

All the rest of the classes that can be built in R are combinations of these six. In the later sections, you will find a list of the most common ones.

Vectors

Vectors are objects that contain elements of only one atomic class. The type of the vector will be the same as the elements it contains (for example, a numeric vector or a character vector). It is important to keep in mind that, as is the case with variables, if a value is added to a vector that does not correspond to the vector type, R will eventually change the vector type in order to adjust it to all the values in the vector instead of throwing an error:

```
> aaa <- numeric(length=5)
> aaa[1] <- 6
> aaa[2] <- 2
> class(aaa)
[1] "numeric"


> aaa[3] <- "a string"
> class(aaa)
[1] "character"
```

As shown in the preceding example, R will try to coerce the vector class in order to make it fit in to the vector. Of course, in this case the first two elements of the vector cannot be used as numbers:

```
> aaa[1] - aaa[2]
Error in aaa[1] - aaa[2] : non-numeric argument to binary operator
```

> The c() function stands for combine and is usually the most comfortable way of generating vectors in R; it generates a vector of the least general class that can support all the input values. For example, if at least one character is passed (and the other elements are, for instance, numbers), the vector will be of the character class and the numbers will all be treated as such.

Lists

Lists are the vectors that support any objects of any class, elemental or non-elemental. It is very common, indeed, that lists will contain other lists within them. In the case of a list, its elements preserve its original class:

```
> aaa <- list()
> aaa[1] <- 4
```

```
> aaa[2] <- 5
> aaa[3] <- "a string"
> aaa
[[1]]
[1] 4


[[2]]
[1] 5


[[3]]
[1] "a string"


> aaa[[2]] - aaa[[1]]
[1] 1
```

Although the selection of elements in lists in R is covered in detail in the *Selecting elements over lists* section of this chapter, it is worth mentioning that to access the elements in the lists by index (the first element, the second element, and so on), double brackets are needed.

Matrices and arrays

Matrices and arrays are special types of vectors. In fact, they are vectors with a dimension attribute. This can be easily tested, as follows:

```
> numeric.vector <- 1:20
> attr(numeric.vector, "dim") <- c(10,2)
> class(numeric.vector)
[1] "matrix"
```

Matrices are special types of arrays that have two dimensions, that is, rows and columns. Alternatively, they can be generated as follows:

```
> numeric.vector <- 1:20
> numeric.vector <- matrix(numeric.vector,10,2)
> class(numeric.vector)
[1] "matrix"
```

Similar to vectors, matrices and arrays contain only elements of the same type. As it was already explained, using `attr(object,"dim")` is equivalent to using `dim(object)`.

Data frames

A data frame is a special type of list, where all the elements of the list have the same length. For this reason, it is presented as an object consisting of *n observations of m variables*. This resembles a two-dimensional matrix structure, with the difference that as it is a list, it can contain elements of different classes. By default, all the functions that read table structures (see the upcoming *Reading data* section) return a data frame.

Additional characteristics of data frame objects can be found at `http://cran.r-project.org/doc/manuals/r-release/R-intro.html#Data-frames`. For further information about indexing data frames, see the *Selecting elements over data frames* section of this chapter.

Factors

A factor is a special class designed for categorical variables. It can be mainly thought of as a numeric code that stands for a character element, which is its label. Technically, it consists of a set of integers (that is, non-decimal numbers) and its corresponding levels (mainly, the label). By default, strings are coerced to factors when data frame objects are created. For this reason, it is important to have a clear understanding of its structure.

In the following example, an `animals` character vector is created and coerced to a factor. This means that every distinct element in the object was changed for a numeric value starting from 1 and assigned a label. In this case, there are three levels with three labels (`dog`, `cat`, and `horse`). If the variable is invoked, R will print the actual values of the labeled vector and all the labels as follows:

```
> animals <- c("dog","cat","dog","horse")
> animals <- as.factor(animals)
> animals
[1] dog    cat    dog    horse
Levels: cat dog horse
```

However, if `animals` is passed to `cat()`, the codes are displayed as follows:

```
> cat(animals)
2 1 2 3
```

When factors are coerced to character, the output is an element of the character class of the labels, and when they are coerced to numeric it is the code:

```
> as.character(animals)
[1] "dog"   "cat"   "dog"   "horse"
> as.numeric(animals)
[1] 2 1 2 3
```

Element selection

Let's now examine how elements can be selected from various class features.

Selecting elements from vectors

At this point in the chapter, you probably already suspect that in order to select specific items from a vector, the selection condition must be enclosed in []．

There are basically three ways of selecting elements from arrays in R. They are as follows:

1. **By index**: A set of integers that indicate the position of the elements to select:

    ```
    > LETTERS[c(1,5,6)]
    [1] "A" "E" "F"
    ```

    LETTERS is a character vector built-in object in R that contains the entire alphabet in upper case. For lower case, use LETTERS.

    Using negative subscripts removes specific elements from an object (unlike in languages such as Python, where it implies reverse order):

    ```
    > LETTERS[-c(1,5,6)]
    [1] "B" "C" "D" "G" "H" "I" "J" "K" "L" "M" "N" "O" "P" "Q" "R"
    "S" "T" "U" "V" "W" "X"
    [22] "Y" "Z"
    ```

    In R, indexing starts at 1 and not at 0.

The reverse order of the vector can be obtained with the `rev()` function:

```
> rev(LETTERS)
[1] "Z" "Y" "X" "W" "V" "U" "T" "S" "R" "Q" "P" "O" "N" "M" "L"
"K" "J" "I" "H" "G" "F"
[22] "E" "D" "C" "B" "A"
```

2. **By name**: The elements in a vector can be named. It is mainly an attribute of its elements. A vector of any class will have an equal length vector of attribute names. When an element does not have a name associated with it, R defaults it to NA:

```
> aaa <- 1:10
> names(aaa) <- LETTERS[1:5]
> names(aaa)
[1] "A" "B" "C" "D" "E" NA NA NA NA NA
```

When a vector has names associated with its elements, they can also be accessed by name:

```
> aaa <- 1:10
> names(aaa) <- LETTERS[1:10]
> aaa[c("A","C","D")]
A C D
1 3 4
```

When a vector has names associated with its values, the names are also printed by default.

3. **By logical vector**: By passing a logical vector, elements matching TRUE are selected and elements matching FALSE are not:

```
> aaa <- 1:5
> aaa[c(T,F,F,T,T)]
[1] 1 4 5
```

 T and F are shortcuts for TRUE and FALSE.

In the case of logical vectors, if the vector passed is shorter than one that is being selected, the logical vector is recycled. This means that it is repeated over the length of the vector sequentially, so if the length of the vector being selected is not a multiple of the logical vector, it will use the necessary elements to apply the logical vector over the whole vector:

```
> aaa[c(T,F)]

[1] 1 3 5
```

The T, F vector is recycled as T, F, T, F, T. In the case of c(F, T), the result is 2, 4 because the logical vector results in F, T, F, T, F:

```
> aaa[c(F,T)]

[1] 2 4
```

Vector recycling is not exclusive to logical vectors. When comparing two vectors, for example, if they differ in length, the shorter one will be recycled in the same way. However, among the three methods of selecting elements from a vector mentioned here, this is the only one where this occurs.

As you may have already realized, in order to select the elements of a vector, another vector is passed inside the brackets.

Lastly, it is worth mentioning that when a non-existing element is selected (when the index number is greater than the length of the vector, it is called by a non-existing name, or the logical vector is larger than the selected vector), NAs are returned. NA denotes a missing value.

When the index number is greater than the length of the vector, you get the following:

```
> aaa <- LETTERS

> aaa[50]

[1] NA
```

When a non-existing name is used, you get the following:

```
> aaa <- 1:10

> names(aaa) <- LETTERS[1:10]

> aaa["Z"]

<NA>

NA
```

In this case, either the value or the name exists, so the vector returns NAs for both the name of the element (enclosed in < >) and for the value itself.

Selecting elements from arrays

The way to select elements from arrays is the same as the preceding method (that is, by index number, by name, and by logical vector) with the sole difference that the selections over the different dimensions of the array are separated by commas. The selection, in the case of the arrays, does not refer to individual elements but to the whole element of that dimension.

For example, if the object was a matrix (that is, a two-dimensional array), then `[c(1,3),c(2,4)]` would be the selection of the first and third rows and the second and fourth columns, this means four values as follows:

```
aaa<-matrix(1:16,4,4)

aaa
##        [,1] [,2] [,3] [,4]
## [1,]    1    5    9   13
## [2,]    2    6   10   14
## [3,]    3    7   11   15
## [4,]    4    8   12   16
```

A matrix of 16 numbers is created, as shown here:

```
aaa[c(1,3),c(2,4)]
##       [,1] [,2]
## [1,]    5   13
## [2,]    7   15
```

This is the selection of first and third row, and second and fourth columns.

However, as the underlying structure of the matrix is a vector, objects can still be selected in the same way as previously explained. This is as follows:

```
> aaa[5]
[1] 5
```

The assignment of names in the arrays is slightly different. As explained previously, to assign names to the elements of a vector, the attribute to modify is names. This is done either via names(object) or attr(object, "names"). In the case of arrays, the attribute that describes the row and column names is dimnames. Unlike names, which is a character vector, dimnames is a list with two elements, a character vector for rows and a character vector for columns.

So in order to assign names to rows or columns, the index has to be specified as follows:

```
> dimnames(aaa) <- LETTERS[1:4]
Error in dimnames(aaa) <- LETTERS[1:4] : 'dimnames' must be a list
```

R throws an error when you try to pass a vector to dimnames.

As it was already mentioned, to access or modify values of a list, double brackets are needed. So in this case, to add names to the rows, the solution would be this:

```
> dimnames(aaa)[[1]] <- LETTERS[1:4]
```

When the result is printed, the names appear on the left, as shown here:

```
aaa
##     [,1] [,2] [,3] [,4]
## A    1    5    9    13
## B    2    6   10    14
## C    3    7   11    15
## D    4    8   12    16
```

The process is exactly the same as in the case of the column names, except for the fact that the index number is 2:

```
> dimnames(aaa)[[2]] <- LETTERS[5:8]
aaa
##     E F  G  H
## A 1 5  9 13
## B 2 6 10 14
## C 3 7 11 15
## D 4 8 12 16
```

In the case of matrices, there are simpler functions to get or assign values to rows and column names, row.names() and colnames(). They are used in the same way:

```
> row.names(aaa) <- LETTERS[1:4]
> colnames(aaa) <- LETTERS[5:8]
```

These two alternatives are equivalent to the ones previously explained. With a named array, the way to access the different vectors is identical:

```
aaa[c("A","C"), c("E","F")]
##   E F
## A 1 5
## C 3 7
```

Lastly, to select all the elements from one of the dimensions, the selection for that dimension must be kept empty, but the comma must be maintained:

```
aaa[1:2,]
##   E F  G  H
## A 1 5  9 13
## B 2 6 10 14
```

The preceding code will select the first two rows and all the columns.

Selecting elements from lists

As it was explained before in this chapter (see the `Lists` section), a list is an object that supports any type of object in its elements. So, there is a need to make a notation difference between the selection of the parts of the list (sublists) and the access to the element itself contained in the list. In this sense, Hadley Wickham gives a perfect explanation:

> "*[selects sub-lists. It always returns a list; if you use it with a single positive integer, it returns a list of length one. [[selects an element within a list.*"

You can get more information at http://adv-r.had.co.nz/Subsetting.html. Have a look at the following snippet:

```
> #List
> list.ex <- list(a=c(1,2,3),b=c("a","b","c"), c =
list(var1="a",var2="b"))
>
> #List of length one
> class(list.ex[2])
[1] "list"
>
> #What is inside the second element of the list
> class(list.ex[[2]])
[1] "character"
```

As they might differ in their respective classes, it is not allowed in R to access multiple elements in a list. So for instance, `list.ex[[1:3]]` is not permitted. Analogously, the elements within the lists can be accessed by name in double brackets:

```
> #List
> list.ex <- list(a=c(1,2,3),b=c("a","b","c"),
c=list(var1="a",var2="b"))
>
> #Access per name
> list.ex[["b"]]
[1] "a" "b" "c"
```

Another way of selecting items over lists when the items are named is using the $ operator. In RStudio, in fact, you can see the named elements of the list by pressing *Tab* after the $ operator:

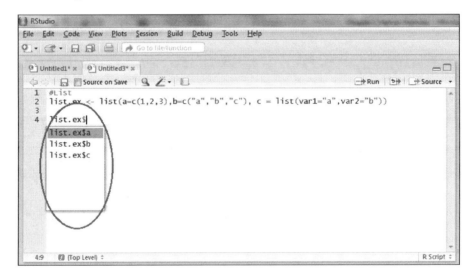

Selecting elements from data frames

As it has been previously explained, a data frame is a special type of list where all its elements have the same length. As such, all the alternatives to selecting elements from lists, naturally, can also be used with data frames:

```
> test.data.frame <-data.frame(Variable1=1:10,Variable2=LETTERS[1:10])
> test.data.frame$Variable1
 [1]  1  2  3  4  5  6  7  8  9 10
> test.data.frame[["Variable1"]]
```

```
 [1]  1  2  3  4  5  6  7  8  9 10
> test.data.frame[[1]]
 [1]  1  2  3  4  5  6  7  8  9 10
```

However, due to its matrix-like structure, R also provides the possibility of matrix-like indexing, as shown here:

```
> test.data.frame[5,1]
[1] 5
> test.data.frame[5,"Variable1"]
[1] 5
> test.data.frame[5,c(T,F)]
[1] 5
```

Finally, it is also possible to select elements over data frames with subset(). This function provides the possibility of selecting observations in the data frame based on conditions related to the variables in it:

```
> subset(test.data.frame, Variable1 >= 8)
   Variable1 Variable2
8          8         H
9          9         I
10        10         J
```

The subset() function also has the possibility of selecting variables from the data frame that are passed with the select argument, which can specify which elements to keep or which to eliminate. In this case, the elements should be preceded by a minus sign. The following example illustrates the function's use:

```
> test.data.frame <- data.frame(Variable1=1:10,Variable2=LETTERS[1:10],
Variable3 = LETTERS[11:20])
> subset(test.data.frame, Variable1 >= 8, select = c(Variable1,
Variable3))
   Variable1 Variable3
8          8         R
9          9         S
10        10         T
> subset(test.data.frame, Variable1 >= 8, select = -Variable2)
   Variable1 Variable3
8          8         R
9          9         S
10        10         T
```

Control structures in R

Control structures in computer programming are statements that decide the execution (or not) of certain pieces of code. In `while` and `if`, they are based on a condition that evaluates to `TRUE` or `FALSE`, and in `for`, the statement is executed for every element of the input sequence.

In R, all the control structures have the same coding pattern, as follows:

```
control_structure(condition or sequence){code block}
```

The if...else block

The following is a small example of an `if...else` block in R. You can play with it by changing the value of `a`:

```
> a <- 5
> if(a > 0){print("a is greater than 0")} else
+ { print("a is smaller than 0")}
[1] "a is greater than 0"
```

 The `else` clause must start in the same line where the `if` clause ends.

With an `else...if` statement, it would be:

```
> a <- 10
> if(a < 0 ){
+    print("a is smaller than 0")} else if(a >= 0 & a <= 5)
+       { print("a is between 0 and 5")} else
+    { print("a is greater than 5")}
[1] "a is greater than 5"
```

The while loop

The use of `while` must be well controlled, as it can lead to infinite or large loops, even causing system collapse. An example of this loop is as follows:

```
> while(a < 4){
+    print(paste("This is iteration",a))
+    a <- a + 1
```

```
+ }
[1] "This is iteration 1"
[1] "This is iteration 2"
[1] "This is iteration 3"
```

The for loop

The `for` loop is a special form of control structure as it does not require an explicit condition. However, it is implicitly given in the length of the sequence passed, that is, it will stop when it comes to its last element in the vector that is passed. These vectors can be of any class.

The following is a loop over a character vector:

```
> vector <- c("aaa","bbb","ccc")
> for(i in vector){
+
+    print(i)
+
+ }
[1] "aaa"
[1] "bbb"
[1] "ccc"
```

The following is a loop over a numeric vector:

```
> numbers <- 1:3
> for(i in numbers){
+
+    print(i + 2)
+
+ }
[1] 3
[1] 4
[1] 5
```

Here, `i` replaces the elements of the loop over the iterations during the execution of the code.

The switch statement

Although `switch()` is not strictly a control structure, it works in the same way as `if()`. In fact, it is an abbreviation of a chain of `if/else...if/else` statements where the condition matches an exact value. Switch has different behaviors and logic based on whether the value that is being evaluated matches a string or a number.

In the case of strings, a default value (the `else` statement) is allowed, while in the case of numbers, it is not. A number in the condition argument implicitly refers to an index. For example, see the following:

```
if(a == 1)
{ print("a is 1")} else if (a == 2)
{print("a is 2")} else if ( a == 3)
{print ("a is 3")}
```

This could be rewritten as shown here:

```
print(switch(a,"a is 1","a is 2","a is 3"))
```

In the case of characters, each of the cases must be explicit, except for the default, as follows:

```
> inp <- "b"
> switch(inp,
+         a=print("inp is a"),
+         b=print("inp is b"),
+         c=print("inp is c"))
[1] "inp is b"
```

The following is an example with a default case:

```
> inp <- "d"
>
> switch(inp,
+         a=print("inp is a"),
+         b=print("inp is b"),
+         c=print("inp is c"),
+         print("inp is not a, b, or c"))
[1] "inp is not a, b, or c"
```

Reading data

The formats and structures in which data comes can be varied. However, thanks to its contributive feature and extensibility, there is a package to load data into R for almost every data structure (at least the standard ones). In order to do this, it is always necessary to use functions that have different argument types according to their nature.

Delimited data

All the delimited formats in R use the same base function, that is, read.table(). This function uses many arguments but most of them have a default value. The following is a list of the most important ones:

- header: If it is set to T, the first row is used to assign the names of the data frame.

- nrows: This gives the amount of rows to be read. If it is set to -1, all rows are read.

- skip: This states how many rows to skip before reading is started.

- encoding: In case the data source contains non-ASCII characters (for example, words in languages different from English), encoding can be passed.

> For information about the rest of the arguments, visit https://stat.ethz.ch/R-manual/R-devel/library/utils/html/read.table.html.

The only non-default argument that this function and its derivatives (read.csv(), read.delim(), and so on) have is file, the path to where the data input file is located. The path can be local or a URL. However, it is usually useful (and safer) to specify the delimiter as read.table, which uses whitespace as a default delimiter:

```
#URL to Iris Dataset
path <- "https://archive.ics.uci.edu/ml/machine-learning-databases/
iris/iris.data"

#Load dataset with generic read.table()
data <- read.table(path, sep=",")
```

The output of this function is a named `data.frame,` as shown here:

```
> class(data)
[1] "data.frame"
```

Reading line by line

The function to read texts line by line is `readLines()`. As in the case of `read.table()`, the only required argument is the file path or a connection object (connection objects will be not covered here, for further information, visit `https://stat.ethz.ch/R-manual/R-devel/library/base/html/connections.html`). The `readLines()` function mainly reads a string and separates it by newline (\n), as follows:

```
#URL to Iris Dataset
path <- "https://archive.ics.uci.edu/ml/machine-learning-databases/
iris/iris.data"

#Load dataset with readLines()
data <- readLines(path)
```

The output of `readLines()` is a character vector whose elements correspond to the lines of the read file, as shown here:

```
> class(data)
[1] "character"
> length(data)
[1] 151
```

Reading a character set

The function to read characters is `readChar()`. In this case, not only the file path or a connection object is needed, but also the number of characters that must be read (the `nchars` argument). If `nchars` is greater than the total number of characters in the string, it will stop at the end of the string, as follows:

```
#URL to Iris Dataset
path <- "https://archive.ics.uci.edu/ml/machine-learning-databases/
iris/iris.data"

#Load dataset with readChar
data <- readChar(path,nchars= 1e5)
```

XeY format is equal to X10^y.

The output of `readChar()` is a character object, which is equal to a character vector of length 1, as the following code shows:

```
> class(data)
[1] "character"
> length(data)
[1] 1
```

Reading JSON

JSON is an acronym that stands for **JavaScript Object Notation** and is basically a non-structured data storage format, which will be discussed later in this book. As functions to read JSON do not come in the default packages, installing new packages is required. The commonly used packages for this purpose are RJSONIO and rjson. Although both the packages return similar things, the main difference between them is that the first one can load data from connections directly but the second one needs an intermediate step to load data into R.

Here's an example with RJSONIO:

```
#Load RJSONIO
library(RJSONIO)

#URL Public API Worldbank Data Catalog in JSON format
url <- "http://api.worldbank.org/v2/datacatalog?format=json"

#Read data directly from url
json <- fromJSON(url)
```

Here's an example with rjson:

```
#Load RJSONIO
library(rjson)

#URL Public API Worldbank Data Catalog in JSON format
url <- "http://api.worldbank.org/v2/datacatalog?format=json"

#Read data with readChar
```

```
raw.json <- readChar(url,nchars=1e6)

#Format into JSON
json <- fromJSON(raw.json)
```

As both the packages share the same function names, the last loaded package will override the function of the other one. In this case, for instance, if rjson is loaded after RJSONIO, fromJSON() will work as defined in rjson and not RJSONIO. In such cases, you will receive this message:

```
library(RJSONIO)
library(rjson)
##
## Attaching package: 'rjson'
##
## The following objects are masked from 'package:RJSONIO':
##
##      fromJSON, toJSON
```

The output in both cases is a list.

Reading XML

XML is another non-structured data storage format and stands for **Extended Markup Language**. Although it has been lately replaced by JSON, XML is still frequently found, for example, in feeds. To read XML files, the XML package is recommended. This package has a large number of functions. The following is an example of how to load XML data into R:

```
#Load XML library
library(XML)

#URL Public API Worldbank Data Catalog in XML format
url <- "http://api.worldbank.org/v2/datacatalog?format=xml"

#Load XML document
xml.obj <- xmlTreeParse(url)
```

The object returned is of the XMLDocument class:

```
> class(xml.obj)
[1] "XMLDocument"        "XMLAbstractDocument"
```

Reading databases – SQL

The packages used to interface with relational databases are RODBC for ODBC connectivity and RJDBC for JDBC. For obvious reasons, it is impossible in this case to refer to a concrete example. In order to use and understand in depth the capabilities of these packages, prior knowledge of ODBC/JDBC is required.

The documentation is available at `http://cran.r-project.org/web/packages/RODBC/RODBC.pdf` and `http://cran.r-project.org/web/packages/RJDBC/RJDBC.pdf`.

Reading data from external sources

For almost every data file in tabular form, there is a package to import it to R. It is out of the scope of this book to go further into this. The most important ones are `xlsx` (for Excel files), `Hmisc` (for SAS and SPSS portable files), and `foreign` (for SAS, SPSS, Stata, Octave, and Weka among others). However, it is always preferred, when possible, to convert any of these files to a standard text file format, such as `.csv` to ensure that unexpected (and sometimes very difficult to solve) problems are avoided.

Summary

In this chapter, you have acquired a solid knowledge of classes, objects, and functions, elements selections in vectors and lists, control structures, and how to read data. These are the fundamentals to start working in R. In the next chapter, useful functions to process and clean data will be covered. These will provide you with useful tools to obtain data from a source, process it in any way desired, and in the end, display it via web applications in Shiny.

In the next chapter, we are going to take a look at different functions and packages for data processing in R.

3
An Introduction to Data Processing in R

In this chapter, basic techniques to fulfill the reorganization of data (cleaning, processing, and so on) will be covered. These will be the key factors while developing web applications with R and Shiny because, unlike traditional web application commercial software, they provide the possibility of performing any operation on your data and consequently, displaying it in the exact way that was imagined with no boundaries. By presenting several useful tools, this chapter will help the reader to gain skills in data manipulation.

The chapter is divided into the following seven sections:

- Sorting elements
- Basic summary functions
- grep and regular expressions
- The apply-like functions
- The `plyr` package
- The `data.table` package
- The `reshape2` package

Sorting elements

There are mainly two functions in the base R package (that is, the package that comes by default when installing R) to display ordered elements—sort() and order().

- sort(): This is a function that returns the passed vector in decreasing or increasing order:

  ```
  > vector1 <- c(2,5,3,4,1)
  > sort(vector1)
  [1] 1 2 3 4 5
  ```

  If the vector passed is of the character type, the function returns it in alphabetical order and if it is logical, it will first return the FALSE elements and then the TRUE elements:

  ```
  > sort(c(T,T,F,F))
  [1] FALSE FALSE TRUE TRUE
  ```

- order(): This returns the index number of the ordered elements according to their values:

  ```
  > vector1 <- c(2,5,3,4,1)
  > order(vector1)
  [1] 5 1 3 4 2
  ```

  In the preceding example, for the vector1 object, the function returns the fifth element first, then the first, then the third, and so on. For character or logical vectors, the criterion is the same as in sort():

  ```
  > sort(vector1,decreasing=T)
  [1] 5 4 3 2 1
  ```

 To return elements in decreasing order in both the sort() and order() functions, include decreasing=T in the function call, as the default is decreasing=F, which means increasing order.

sort() versus order()

To obtain an identical result of `sort(object)` with `order()`, the object could be indexed by the output of its `order()` function:

```
> vector1[order(vector1)]
[1] 1 2 3 4 5
```

As explained in the previous chapter, the elements of a vector can be accessed by index numbers, and as `order()` returns the index numbers according to their value, indexing a vector by its `order()` output will result in an ordered vector.

Unlike `sort()`, `order()` can handle multiple input vectors where ordering criteria is applied in the order the vectors are passed. For example, if there was a tie in the ordering by the first criteria, the second vector will be used:

```
> vector1 <- c(2,2,3,3,1)
> vector2 <- c(2,5,4,3,1)
> order(vector1,vector2,decreasing = c(T,F))
[1] 3 4 2 1 5
```

Note that with multiple vectors, a logical vector has to be passed to the decreasing argument. As it happens with element selection, in the case the length of the logical vector is smaller than the number of vectors being ordered, the logical vector will be recycled, as explained in *Chapter 2, First Steps towards Programming in R*.

The `order()` function is particularly useful to order matrices or data frames by indexing per row by the output of the order based upon any of its columns:

```
> data(iris)
> names(iris)
[1] "Sepal.Length" "Sepal.Width" "Petal.Length" "Petal.Width" "Species"
> iris.ordered <- iris[order(iris$Sepal.Length, iris$Sepal.Width),]
```

 Iris is a dataset that comes from Sir Ronald Fisher's investigation in 1936 about different species of Iris. It is considered a standard dataset and is available in the R base package. It can be loaded just by typing `data(iris)`.

After loading the `iris` data frame object, a new `iris.ordered` object is created. It is the same dataset as `iris` but ordered by `Sepal.Length` and `Sepal.Width` as the `order` function returns the corresponding indexes, which are then applied to the `iris` dataset. Note that, as it is a data frame, the indexing has a comma that separates rows from columns (in the case of data frames, observations from variables). As there is nothing after the comma, R returns all the variables:

	row.names	Sepal.Length	Sepal.Width	Petal.Length	Petal.Width	Species
1	14	4.3	3.0	1.1	0.1	setosa
2	9	4.4	2.9	1.4	0.2	setosa
3	39	4.4	3.0	1.3	0.2	setosa
4	43	4.4	3.2	1.3	0.2	setosa
5	42	4.5	2.3	1.3	0.3	setosa
6	4	4.6	3.1	1.5	0.2	setosa
7	48	4.6	3.2	1.4	0.2	setosa
8	7	4.6	3.4	1.4	0.3	setosa
9	23	4.6	3.6	1.0	0.2	setosa
10	3	4.7	3.2	1.3	0.2	setosa
11	30	4.7	3.2	1.6	0.2	setosa
12	13	4.8	3.0	1.4	0.1	setosa
13	46	4.8	3.0	1.4	0.3	setosa
14	31	4.8	3.1	1.6	0.2	setosa

iris.ordered × — 150 observations of 5 variables

 Unlike other languages, dots in R are allowed in variable, column, or row names.

In conclusion, `order()` particularly is a very useful function, especially because it is the best way to order data frames and matrices.

Basic summary functions

In this section, `table()` and `aggregate()` will be covered. They are basic processing functions that come in the base package.

- `table()`: This creates a contingency table with the specified vectors. Although its output is of the table type, it works similar to an array:

```
sample.data <-data.frame(var1 =rep(c("Male","Female"),10), var2
=rep(c("A","B","C","D")))

example.table<-table(sample.data$var1, sample.data$var2)

example.table

##
```

```
##             A B C D
##    Female 0 5 0 5
##    Male   5 0 5 0
example.table[2,2]
## [1] 0
```

The output of `table()` can be indexed in the same way as an array.

- `aggregate()`: This performs one or more functions over a vector split by a factor variable. `aggregate()` has basically two ways of usage:

  ○ **With vectors**: One or more vectors are passed to the x argument while one or more factor vectors are passed in the by argument. FUN is the aggregation function to be used:

  ```
  > data(iris)
  > aggregate(iris$Sepal.Length, by=list(iris$Species),
  FUN="mean")
  Group.1 x
  1 setosa 5.006
  2 versicolor 5.936
  3 virginica 6.588
  ```

  ○ **Through formula objects**: Instead of specifying a vector and a by list, this information can be included in a formula object. Additionally, when using a formula object, it is not necessary to constantly refer to the `data.frame` object being used. In case the variables that are used come from `data.frame`, they can be specified in the data argument.

  With one factor, without the data argument:

  ```
  > aggregate(iris$Sepal.Length ~ iris$Species, FUN="mean")
  ```

  With one factor, with the data argument:

  ```
  aggregate(Sepal.Length ~Species, data = iris, FUN ="mean")
  ##        Species Sepal.Length
  ## 1       setosa        5.006
  ## 2 versicolor        5.936
  ## 3   virginica        6.588
  ```

With two factors—as there is no other factor variable, a variable letter is added:

```
iris$letter <-LETTERS[1:5]
aggregate(Sepal.Length ~Species +letter, data = iris, FUN
="mean")
##          Species letter Sepal.Length
## 1         setosa      A         5.16
## 2     versicolor      A         5.96
## 3      virginica      A         6.94
## 4         setosa      B         5.03
## 5     versicolor      B         6.11
## 6      virginica      B         6.28
## 7         setosa      C         4.85
## 8     versicolor      C         6.07
## 9      virginica      C         6.78
## 10        setosa      D         4.95
## 11    versicolor      D         5.82
## 12     virginica      D         6.44
## 13        setosa      E         5.04
## 14    versicolor      E         5.72
## 15     virginica      E         6.50
```

Compute the mean of all variables by species:

```
data(iris)
aggregate(. ~Species, data = iris, FUN ="mean")
##   Species Sepal.Length Sepal.Width Petal.Length Petal.Width
## 1    setosa        5.006       3.428        1.462       0.246
## 2 versicolor       5.936       2.770        4.260       1.326
## 3  virginica       6.588       2.974        5.552       2.026
```

Formula objects are of the x ~ y form where, in `aggregate()`, x is the vector over which the aggregation functions will be applied and y is the splitting factor. To combine the elements on the right-hand side, + is used. Formula objects are also very commonly used in modeling, where x is the variable to model and y is the predictor. Lastly, if all variables should be included in one of the sides (except for the ones specified on the other side) they can be abbreviated with a dot.

grep and regular expressions

grep() in R works exactly as it does in every UNIX-based operating system. Closely related to grep() (in fact, R groups them together and treats them as a group of functions), various other functions can be found. In this section, only grepl(), gregexpr(), and gsub() will be examined. One thing that all these functions have in common is that they perform an action based on a string pattern. The description of the functions are as follows:

- grep(): This returns the indexes of the elements in a vector that match a string pattern. If the value is set to TRUE, it returns the values instead of the indexes.

- grepl(): This returns a logical vector of the same length as the input vector, denoting whether the sought pattern was found or not.

- gsub(): This substitutes the pattern for the replacement argument in the specified vector.

- gregexpr(): This returns a list consisting of the vectors of starting positions that specify where the pattern was matched in the text in addition to the length of that match.

A brief introduction to regular expressions

All these functions implement regular expressions. Regular expressions are strings that represent string patterns. In R, they do not differ very much from Perl standard (see Perl Compatible Regular Expressions for more information). However, there are some differences. This is the reason why the logical argument of Perl can be specified in every function in R that uses regular expressions. This option is normally defaulted to FALSE.

These patterns can vary from the following:

- Sets
- Non-printable characters
- Negation
- Alternation
- Quantifiers
- Anchors
- Expressions
- Escapes

Sets

Sets are a group of characters enclosed by []. This means that the sought pattern can meet any of the characters contained inside the brackets. Letters can be abbreviated by determining a range with a hyphen. For example, a-e would match a, b, c, d, and e. Analogously, numbers can be abbreviated in the same way:

```
> gregexpr("[a-z]", "string 01 A")
[[1]]
[1] 1 2 3 4 5 6
attr(,"match.length")
[1] 1 1 1 1 1 1
attr(,"useBytes")
[1] TRUE
```

The [a-z] pattern is matched at the 1, 2, 3, 4, 5, and 6 positions in the string 01 A string, and the length of all these matches 1. (In this case, it could not have been greater than this because the pattern will match only elements of length 1. For further details, see the *Quantifiers* section of this chapter.) The space and the numbers are not matched because the pattern only matches letters from a-z in lower case.

Within a set, more than one abbreviation can be used. In fact, anything can be included. The logic would remain the same, that is, it will recover anything that matches the specified set. Back to the example, if instead of [a-z], the pattern was [a-z0], the result would be as follows:

```
> gregexpr("[a-z0]", "string 01 A")
[[1]]
[1] 1 2 3 4 5 6 8
attr(,"match.length")
[1] 1 1 1 1 1 1 1
attr(,"useBytes")
[1] TRUE
```

The eighth character (0) is matched.

Shortcuts

R provides a series of shortcuts to work with regular expressions. They can be found at http://stat.ethz.ch/R-manual/R-devel/library/base/html/regex.html. They are mainly common groups of characters and work the same as any other abbreviation.

The following is the same example but with [[:alnum:]] (that is, alphanumeric characters) as pattern:

```
> gregexpr("[[:alnum:]]", "string 01 A")
[[1]]
[1] 1 2 3 4 5 6 8 9 11
attr(,"match.length")
[1] 1 1 1 1 1 1 1 1 1
attr(,"useBytes")
[1] TRUE
```

The pattern matches all the characters except the spaces.

> Notice that the use of double brackets responds to the fact that the set must be enclosed in brackets and the abbreviation also has a bracket structure. In fact, something like [[:alnum:]_] (a pattern that matches any character or digit plus the _ sign) is also possible.

Dot

The dot matches any character except for **newline** (newline is a non-printable character, for further information see the next item in this section). Unlike the other expressions seen previously, the dot character does not need to be enclosed in []:

```
> gregexpr(".", "string 01 A")
[[1]]
[1] 1 2 3 4 5 6 7 8 9 10 11
attr(,"match.length")
[1] 1 1 1 1 1 1 1 1 1 1 1
attr(,"useBytes")
[1] TRUE
```

Dot matches all the characters in the string.

Non-printable characters

Non-printable characters are standard special sets of characters that indicate something about the text but are not actually printed. Among them, the most important ones are *Tab*, newline, and carriage return. To match them in R, the regular expressions must be specified with a double backslash:

```
> gregexpr("\\n", "string 01
+               A")
[[1]]
[1] 10
attr(,"match.length")
[1] 1
attr(,"useBytes")
[1] TRUE
```

Negation

The regular expressions also permit negation. This is denoted by a ^ within the set (that is, inside the brackets). Consequently, they would match everything but the specified negated pattern:

```
> gregexpr("[^a-z]", "string 01 A")
[[1]]
[1] 7 8 9 10 11
attr(,"match.length")
[1] 1 1 1 1 1
attr(,"useBytes")
[1] TRUE
```

Alternation

The character for alternation is |. Its use is similar to the use of or in any language:

```
> gregexpr("r|n", "string 01 A")
[[1]]
[1] 3 5
attr(,"match.length")
[1] 1 1
attr(,"useBytes")
[1] TRUE
```

The pattern r|n matches positions 3 and 5.

Quantifiers

Quantifiers express the number of times that the subpattern should be repeated. Its syntax is {min,max}, where min and max denote the minimum and maximum times the subpattern can be repeated respectively:

```
> gregexpr("[a-z]{2,4}", "string 01 A")
[[1]]
[1] 1 5
attr(,"match.length")
[1] 4 2
attr(,"useBytes")
[1] TRUE
```

There are two important things to consider in this example—firstly, the engine will always try to match the largest string possible. So, if the quantifier is set to {2,4}, the engine will try to match a 4-character string. Secondly, the matches do not overlap, this is the reason why there is no 4 length match at position 2.

Special quantifiers

There are special characters that denote quantity, such as *, ?, and +. The asterisk denotes that the preceding pattern can match 0 to infinite times, the question mark implies optionality, which is equivalent to saying that the preceding pattern can be matched 0 or 1 times, and finally, the plus means that the preceding pattern can match 1 to infinite times.

Anchors

Anchors specify the starting and ending point of the matches. They are expressed with the ^ and $ signs respectively. For example, the tri pattern is matched with string and triangle but ^tri is matched only with *triangle*:

```
> grep("tri", c("string","triangle"), value=T)
[1] "string" "triangle"
> grep("^tri", c("string","triangle"), value=T)
[1] "triangle"
```

The combination of both anchors results in an exact match of the pattern, as it specifies where it starts and where it ends:

```
> grep("^triangle", c("string","triangle","triangles"), value=T)
[1] "triangle" "triangles"
```

The `^triangle` pattern matches `triangle` and `triangles` because it only specifies the beginning of the string. However, the `^triangle$` pattern only matches the `triangle` string:

```
> grep("^triangle$", c("string","triangle","triangles"), value=T)
[1] "triangle"
```

Expressions

Imagine a situation where a pattern must be used that matches any string starting with `pri` or `tri`. From what we have seen so far, the first attempt would be something like `^pri|tri`. However, this would not give the desired outcome:

```
> grep("^pri|tri", c("triangle","triangles","price","priority","string"),
value=T)
[1] "triangle" "triangles" "price" "priority" "string"
```

Here, `string` is matched, although it does not start with `tri` or `pri`. This is actually because the regex in the preceding code is expressing *a string starting with pri or containing tri*. In order to return only strings beginning with `pri` or `tri`, an expression must be used, that is, something that denotes that all the blocks must be evaluated together. This is done by enclosing the expression in parentheses:

```
> grep("^(pri|tri)", c("triangle","triangles","price","priority","stri
ng"), value=T)
[1] "triangle" "triangles" "price" "priority"
```

Escapes

When the pattern must include one of the special characters (dots, question marks, pluses, and so on) and not interpret them in their functions, they must be escaped (that is, deprived from their original meaning in regular expressions and treated as a normal character) with \\ in R:

```
> gregexpr("\\?","what is this?")
[[1]]
[1] 13
attr(,"match.length")
[1] 1
attr(,"useBytes")
[1] TRUE
```

Examples

After this extended explanation of regular expressions, let's look at some commented examples.

Example 1

This example is to find phone numbers within a string vector, with and without a hyphen, and with or without international code (+1 for USA, for example). It is assumed that the country code is separated from the phone number by a space; the prefix is 3 digits long and the suffix is 4 digits long:

```
> numbers <- c("+1 453-
2341","5342673","55578274982","74683029873","25","+442 5421611")
> grep("^(\\+[0-9]+\\s)?[0-9]{3}\\-?[0-9]{4}$",numbers,value=T)
[1] "+1 453-2341" "5342673" "+442 5421611"
```

For this example, the pattern should match an optional starting country code, which is the plus sign (escaped because it was sought literally), numbers (no matter how many), and a space (\\s). As the entire subpattern is optional, it is followed by ?. After this, the pattern looks for three numbers, an optional hyphen, and finally four more numbers.

The anchors at the beginning and at the end match only those strings that had exactly seven numbers because they begin with 3 (and eventually a country code) and end with 4. In the case that one of the anchors was not included, the result would be as follows:

```
> grep("^(\\+[0-9]+\\s)?[0-9]{3}\\-?[0-9]{4}",numbers,value=T)
[1] "+1 453-2341" "5342673" "55578274982" "74683029873" "+442 5421611"
```

The third and fourth elements of the output were matched because they do have three and then four digits inside (this means, they have seven or more).

Example 2

Another task that could be fulfilled with regular expressions is finding, for example, entire sentences that are questions within a text. In this case, it is assumed that punctuation is respected, that is, a capital letter is used after the beginning of a sentence and that there is a space after each stop:

```
> example.text <- "This is a text. What is this exactly? A text. Are you
sure?"
> greps <- gregexpr("\\s[A-Z]{1}[^\\?\\.]*\\?",example.text)
```

```
> regmatches(example.text,greps)
[[1]]
[1] " What is this exactly?" " Are you sure?"
```

 regmatches() is a very useful function that returns the text matched by gregexpr() by passing the original text and the gregexpr() output.

This regular expression would be read as follows: a space, one capital letter, anything but a question mark or a stop repeated zero or more times, and finally a question mark. It is interesting to note what happens if "anything but a question mark or a stop" is replaced by "anything":

```
> example.text <- "This is a text. What is this exactly? A text. Are you
sure?"
> greps <- gregexpr("\\s[A-Z]{1}.*\\?",example.text)
> regmatches(example.text,greps)
[[1]]
[1] " What is this exactly? A text. Are you sure?"
```

There is only one match that starts at the beginning of the question but ends at the end of the original string. As `.*` matches any printable character, it also matches ? and .. In this case, it will still be matching characters until the end of the string. On the contrary, by specifying that `.` and ? are not desired, the `[^\\?\\.]*` subpattern stops at the question mark, which is then matched with `\\?`. There is a very complete and clear explanation of this at `http://www.regular-expressions.info/repeat.html`.

The lapply, vapply, sapply, and apply functions

These functions are equivalent to a `for-each` loop with the advantage that they are much more efficient in terms of performance. Basically, the function is applied over every item in a vectorized object. Its main structure is:

```
function(object_to_iterate_on, function, additional_
arguments(separated by commas))
```

`vapply()` and `apply()` have additional arguments that will be covered in detail in the expanded explanations of these functions.

The function argument can be an already defined function (with its arguments), as follows:

```
sample.list <- list(a=runif(100,0,1), b=runif(500,0,100),
c=runif(35,0,200))
sapply(sample.list, quantile, probs=0.75)
##        a.75%        b.75%        c.75%
##    0.7145661   77.4817679 158.9351519
```

Also, the function can be defined within the same apply-function call (these types of functions are called anonymous functions), as follows:

```
sapply(sample.list, function(x) round(sum(x+2)))
##      a       b       c
##    250   27235    3867
```

In this example, a function is defined (sum 2 to the entire vector and then round it). Eventually, the first function could also be rewritten in this way:

```
> sapply(sample.list, function(x) quantile(x,probs=0.75))
```

The following are the differences between each function:

- `lapply()`: In this, a vector is passed and the output is returned in a list.
- `sapply()`: In this, a vector is passed and the output's class is defined by the function.
- `vapply()`: In this, a vector and a format specification is passed and the output is returned in the specified format.
- `apply()`: In this, an array and a direction (mainly, row-wise or column-wise) is passed, and the output is guessed by the function. It is important to consider that in the case of `apply()`, a data frame (instead of a matrix) can be passed but it is coerced to a matrix with the corresponding class transformation. This is particularly important if the function that is to be applied uses elements of different classes.

Examples

The following are a few examples:

```
> data(iris)
> apply(iris,1, function(x) as.numeric(x["Sepal.Width"]) +
as.numeric(x["Sepal.Length"]) + 3)
```

```
[1] 11.6 10.9 10.9 10.7 11.6 12.3 11.0 11.4 10.3 11.0 12.1 11.2 10.8 10.3
12.8 13.1
[17] 12.3 11.6 12.5 11.9 11.8 11.8 11.2 11.4 11.2 11.0 11.4 11.7 11.6
10.9 10.9 11.8
[33] 12.3 12.7 11.0 11.2 12.0 11.5 10.4 11.5 11.5 9.8 10.6 11.5 11.9 10.8
11.9 10.8
[49] 12.0 11.3 13.2 12.6 13.0 10.8 12.3 11.5 12.6 10.3 12.5 10.9 10.0
11.9 11.2 12.0
[65] 11.5 12.8 11.6 11.5 11.4 11.1 12.1 11.9 11.8 11.9 12.3 12.6 12.6
12.7 11.9 11.3
[81] 10.9 10.9 11.5 11.7 11.4 12.4 12.8 11.6 11.6 11.0 11.1 12.1 11.4
10.3 11.3 11.7
[97] 11.6 12.1 10.6 11.5 12.6 11.5 13.1 12.2 12.5 13.6 10.4 13.2 12.2
13.8 12.7 12.1
[113] 12.8 11.2 11.6 12.6 12.5 14.5 13.3 11.2 13.1 11.4 13.5 12.0 13.0
13.4 12.0 12.1
[129] 12.2 13.2 13.2 14.7 12.2 12.1 11.7 13.7 12.7 12.5 12.0 13.0 12.8
13.0 11.5 13.0
[145] 13.0 12.7 11.8 12.5 12.6 11.9
```

As it has been mentioned before, `apply` transforms the data frame to a matrix, which, by definition, has a unique class. The number 1 in the margin argument (the direction) implies that the function application is done per row. In this case, as the `Species` variable is a character, the dataset is coerced to a character matrix. This is the reason why, in the function call, the `Sepal.Width` variable must be transformed to a numeric value.

In this example, the column name was used to specify which columns were to be used. Alternatively, index numbers can be also used:

```
> names(iris)
[1] "Sepal.Length" "Sepal.Width" "Petal.Length" "Petal.Width" "Species"
> apply(iris,1, function(x) as.numeric(x[2]) + as.numeric(x[1]) + 3)
```

This is what happens if the variables are not transformed to their corresponding classes:

```
> apply(iris,1, function(x) x[2] + x[1] + 3)
Error in x[2] + x[1] : non-numeric argument to binary operator
```

R, basically, throws an error because it does not recognize the arguments as numbers.

However, if the data frame contains only numeric values, it is coerced to a numeric matrix. The following is an explanation of the use of `apply` column-wise without needing to cast the variables inside the function:

```
apply(iris[,1:4], 2, mean)
## Sepal.Length  Sepal.Width Petal.Length  Petal.Width
##     5.843333     3.057333     3.758000     1.199333
```

From the `iris` dataset, the mean for each column except the species is calculated. However, as the species is not included in the matrix argument, it is coerced to a numeric matrix as the other four variables are numeric. If the complete dataset was passed, it would throw an error.

plyr

The logic of `plyr` is very similar to `aggregate()` and `apply()`. In fact, the title of the package is *Tools for splitting, applying, and combining data.*

Its main functions can be easily understood since they are all named for its input and output objects, based upon the following references:

- d: This is for a data frame
- a: This is for an array
- l: This is for a list
- m: This is for a data frame or an array (column-wise, only as input)
- _: This is for a function's guess (only for outputs)

So, for instance, `laply` receives a list and returns an array, `ddply` receives a data frame and returns a data frame, and so on.

Although the package has a wide variety of functions available, all the ones that have a data frame as input are the most important ones (also, the ones starting with d). The following are a few of its usage:

```
ddply(iris,.(Species), summarize, indicator1=quantile(Sepal.Length,0.75),
indicator2=sum(Sepal.Width)/sum(Petal.Length))
##      Species indicator1 indicator2
## 1     setosa        5.2  2.3447332
## 2 versicolor        6.3  0.6502347
## 3  virginica        6.9  0.5356628
```

```
dlply(iris,.(Species), summarize, indicator1=quantile(Sepal.Length,0.75),
indicator2=sum(Sepal.Width)/sum(Petal.Length))
## $setosa
##    indicator1 indicator2
## 1         5.2   2.344733
##
## $versicolor
##    indicator1 indicator2
## 1         6.3  0.6502347
##
## $virginica
##    indicator1 indicator2
## 1         6.9  0.5356628
##
## attr(,"split_type")
## [1] "data.frame"
## attr(,"split_labels")
##        Species
## 1       setosa
## 2   versicolor
## 3    virginica
```

For further information on the use of plyr, visit its manual at http://cran.r-project.org/web/packages/plyr/plyr.pdf.

The data.table package

data.table is a revolutionary package in R because it uses a new approach to data processing that results in a much faster execution time. However, it has a drawback that it uses a syntax that, although easy to understand, differs considerably from the normal R syntax.

Mainly, every operation in a data table is done inside brackets that normally refer to dimensions in arrays or data frames:

```
data.table.object[operations over rows, operations over columns, by]
```

In the preceding code snippet, by is optional. The columns can be selected either by name or column index. However, for this last option, the with=FALSE argument has to be added:

```
> data(iris)
> iris <- data.table(iris)
> iris[,2,with=F]
Sepal.Width
1:  3.5
2:  3.0
3:  3.2
4:  3.1
5:  3.6
---
146:  3.0
147:  2.5
148:  3.0
149:  3.4
150:  3.0
```

Data table objects are also printed differently. Data table also has the functionality of adding new variables to the object without any need to rename it using the `:=` operator:

```
> names(iris)
[1] "Sepal.Length" "Sepal.Width" "Petal.Length" "Petal.Width" "Species"
> iris[,ratio:=Sepal.Length/Sepal.Width]
> names(iris)
[1] "Sepal.Length" "Sepal.Width" "Petal.Length" "Petal.Width" "Species"
[6] "ratio"
```

Note that there is no variable assignment during the creation of the variable ratio. The `:=` operator creates the variable implicitly in the same object, as follows:

```
> iris[Sepal.Length >= 5.1, median(Petal.Width), by=list(Species)]
Species V1
1: setosa 0.2
2: versicolor 1.3
3: virginica 2.0
```

In this example, the median of `Petal Width` by species with a `Sepal Length` over `5.1` is calculated.

Definitely, a good use of this can improve the performance of data processing tasks, and this can be crucial for dashboards to provide a fast response in real time. However, this section is just a very general overview of data table as it is not the aim of the book to go deeper into these topics. For this reason, the reader is highly encouraged to dive deep into data table to exploit all its potential.

reshape2

reshape2 is a package that consists mainly of two functions: melt and dcast/acast. Generally, it could be said that melt() transforms one row to multiple and shorter rows while dcast() and acast() do exactly the opposite.

The melt() function, basically, transforms one row of data to many by pivoting a set of variables (the measure variables) over a set of other variables (the id variables). The function is called as follows:

```
melt(dataset,id.vars,measure.vars,variable_name)
```

The id variables are usually factors or characters while the measure variables are the numeric ones. In fact, this is the behavior by default if none of the arguments are specified. variable_name is the name that adopts the column where the variables are specified (variable by default):

```
> library(reshape2)
> data(iris)
> melt(iris)
Using Species as id variables
Species         variable     value
1 setosa    Sepal.Length    5.1
2 setosa    Sepal.Length    4.9
3 setosa    Sepal.Length    4.7
4 setosa    Sepal.Length    4.6
5 setosa    Sepal.Length    5.0
6 setosa    Sepal.Length    5.4
7 setosa    Sepal.Length    4.6
8 setosa    Sepal.Length    5.0
```

(Here, the output is cut.)

As can be seen, in the `iris` dataset, `melt()` by default chooses `Species` as the `id` variable and all the others as the measure variables. Then the output of this function is every possible combination of the `id` variables with the measure variables and its corresponding value. The `variable_name` value remained as default but it could have been changed.

As it was previously mentioned, `dcast()` is exactly the opposite function; it transforms multiple rows to one row. The way in which it performs such an operation depends on the specified summarizing function. Although `dcast()` has many other arguments that can be passed, it could be summarized to the following:

```
dcast(data, formula, fun.aggregate = NULL,
value.var = guess_value(data))
```

`formula` is a formula object exactly as in `aggregate`. The aggregating function has the same behavior as in `apply` functions, and it can also be specified within the function call. If not specified, it is defaulted to length (that is, frequency). `value.var` is the variable from which the values to perform the aggregation are taken. When not specified, the function makes a guess:

```
data(iris)
molten.iris <- melt(iris)
## Using Species as id variables
dcast(molten.iris, variable~Species, fun.aggregate= sum)
##          variable  setosa  versicolor  virginica
## 1 Sepal.Length   250.3       296.8      329.4
## 2  Sepal.Width   171.4       138.5      148.7
## 3 Petal.Length    73.1       213.0      277.6
## 4  Petal.Width    12.3        66.3      101.3
```

The dataset used for this `dcast` call is the molten data and the function used is `sum`. The `value.var` argument is guessed. In this case, however, there is only one value variable:

```
data(iris)
molten.iris <- melt(iris)
## Using Species as id variables
dcast(molten.iris, variable~Species, fun.aggregate= function(x) sum(x+2))
##          variable  setosa  versicolor  virginica
## 1 Sepal.Length   350.3       396.8      429.4
## 2  Sepal.Width   271.4       238.5      248.7
## 3 Petal.Length   173.1       313.0      377.6
## 4  Petal.Width   112.3       166.3      201.3
```

In this case, the `aggregate` function is defined within the `dcast` call.

Summary

In this chapter, you acquired a general knowledge of useful packages intended to process data. This is particularly useful while creating web applications in Shiny because it will make a difference to traditional web application software; in R, if you can code it, you can display the data in any way you want. To accomplish this, a good background in data processing is essential.

This is the last chapter dedicated to the issues of R that are crucial to building a web application successfully. The next chapters will be dedicated to different Shiny-related tasks. *Chapter 4, Shiny Structure – Reactivity Concepts*, provides a general explanation of the fundamentals of Shiny, especially the concept of reactivity.

4
Shiny Structure – Reactivity Concepts

Before diving deep into the different possibilities that Shiny provides, it is necessary to have a clear understanding of what Shiny is. For this reason, this chapter covers its central concepts with a special focus on reactivity and explains the structure of their implementation.

In short, we will cover the following topics:

- Shiny as a package
- An introduction to `server.R` and `UI.R`
- The concept of reactivity
- Reactive independent processes within an application
- An introduction to `global.R`
- Running a Shiny web application
- An overview of simple examples

Shiny as a package

In *Chapter 1, Introducing R, RStudio, and Shiny,* we learned that Shiny is a package. Packages in R, in most cases, are a collection of functions (in some cases, also datasets) that serve certain objectives. For example, the `glm` package provides the necessary functions to run general linear models. Packages can also use functions from other packages. In this case, it is said that these packages depend on the package/s that contain the functions that are being used.

Shiny is then a package that contains a set of functions to build web applications within R. However, Shiny is a special package in the following two ways:

- Firstly, for the correct use of its functions, it is necessary to organize the files in a specific structure

- Secondly, the syntax of its functions is also slightly different

An introduction to server.R and UI.R

One of the special requisites to build web applications with Shiny is either the inclusion of, at least, the server.R and UI.R files or the inclusion of app.R, which should contain the equivalent codes of both UI.R and server.R. Shiny searches for these files to run the application.

UI.R stands for User Interface. In fact, UI.R is the file where the different parts of the application's frontend (that is, what the end users see) is defined. server.R, on the contrary, is the backend or the engine of the application, that is, where the data is processed.

As in any other web application, the Shiny-based applications have an underlying input-output concept where the user inserts information (input) and gets something back (output). However, in most cases, the input and output are displayed in the same window. In this sense, Shiny is very intuitive as its UI/server structure responds somehow to this natural idea: everything that the user sees goes under UI.R, and everything that the user does not see goes under server.R.

In a schematic view, the information flow could be summarized as follows:

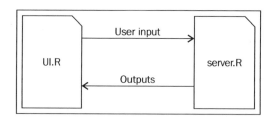

In depth, the following are the steps:

1. The user gives an input to the interface generated by UI.R.

2. The input is passed to server.R. This step does not need to be programmed. Shiny provides the connectivity between the created interface and the R engine.

3. The data is processed in server.R.

4. `server.R` returns an output.

5. The output is passed to the browser. As in step 2, this is done by the Shiny framework and does not need extra programming.

6. The output is displayed as programmed in `UI.R`.

UI.R as a JavaScript/HTML wrapper

`UI.R` is basically a JavaScript/HTML wrapper. This means that some functions in the Shiny package transform the R code to HTML/JavaScript, readable by a web browser. These functions are mostly called within other functions, and there is no need for the programmer to explicitly call them. In fact, as it will be seen afterwards, `UI.R` can be replaced by an HTML document.

Including HTML within UI.R

Apart from the possibility of replacing `UI.R` with an HTML document, Shiny also enables the programmer to insert an HTML code within `UI.R`. As a result, images, different fonts, and more could be included without any need to write an HTML code. Normally, the tags are enclosed in a function.

For example, to insert an image instead of `<img>...</img>`, there is an `img()` function. The next chapter will cover in depth the tagging possibilities within Shiny.

The concept of reactivity

Reactivity is the main concept that underlies the Shiny structure. Basically, this means that an object changes depending on the changes of another object. This concept is intimately related to the input/output relationship. In other words, the output object reacts (changes) whenever the input changes.

For example, let's think of an application that counts the number of words in the phrase that has been passed. It would look similar to this:

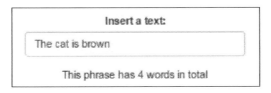

In this case, whenever the phrase passed to the textbox changes, the text below the textbox changes. The reaction process automatically and instantly occurs by default. This means that, unless explicitly told otherwise, the re-execution will take place immediately. For example, if the phrases change, an order is automatically triggered to re-execute the script in `server.R` and consequently, to change the text (that is, the output). To sum it up, the reactive process starts when the input changes and finishes when the output is updated.

Of course, this instant re-execution might not be desired in many cases. For instance, if the execution of `server.R` requires a high consumption of resources and/or the execution times are very long. As it will be seen in *Chapter 7, Advanced Functions in Shiny*, a button that delays the execution of `server.R` script until the button is hit can be included. In this case, for instance, the user could change multiple inputs. This will cause a sole `server.R` re-execution and consequently, a sole output change.

In practice, most of the applications tend to have multiple outputs. Sometimes, the processes to generate some of them have certain things in common. Back to the previous example, imagine that, apart from an output that shows the number of words, we have a second output that shows which is the longest word and how many characters it has. The following screenshot shows how this would look like:

Insert a text:

The cat is brown

This phrase has 4 words in total
brown is the longest word and has 5 characters

Both the outputs take the same input but process it differently. Let's see what each of them does:

- Word counter:
    - Split the passed string (that is, the input) by spaces (we assume that a single space is the word delimiter)
    - Count how many elements were obtained

- Longest word and amount of characters:
    - Split the passed string (that is, the input) by spaces
    - Calculate how many characters each of the obtained elements have
    - Select the highest value in the preceding step
    - Select the element that has the highest value

Although being different, both output generation processes have the first step in common. In this case, instead of repeating the same process for both outputs, Shiny provides the possibility of executing this process only once by generating intermediate objects between the input (the passed phrase) and the outputs. These objects are reactive, but they also cause reaction for the objects that depend on them, which can be the outputs (that is, the final stages of reactivity) or other intermediate objects.

Generating intermediate objects has two main advantages. Firstly, the object is reprocessed only once and used by all the elements that depend on it instead of having the same piece of code executed multiple times. Secondly, this avoids code repetition, which makes it much easier to maintain.

With this same idea of avoiding unnecessary process repetitions in our application, the next section will explain other scenarios where this can happen and how it can be prevented.

Reactive independent processes within an application

Let's imagine an application that loads the `iris` dataset and returns the mean and median of numeric variables based upon the species selected. With the elements seen so far, the output generation process would consist of the following:

- Load the `iris` dataset
- Subset the dataset with the species selected
- Calculate the mean for each variable
- Calculate the median for each variable
- Output the mean and median

As it has been explained before, every reactive element (like outputs) are re-executed whenever an input changes. So, in this case, these five processes would be in constant re-execution.

However, there is an evident issue in this situation: the dataset is always the same one, so the exact same operation is done every time an input changes. The underlying problem is that the load of the iris dataset does not actually depend on the input passed. In other words, it is independent from the application's reactive process.

Shiny provides, basically, two alternatives to write processes outside a reactive context, by coding it either inside `server.R` but prior to the function call that initializes the application, as it is explained in the *Example 3 – loading data outside reactive context* section, or in `global.R`.

An introduction to global.R

`global.R` is a script that is executed before the application launch. For this reason, it can include the same pieces of code to execute the reactive independent processes as previously explained, but it also has an additional capability: the objects generated in `global.R` can be used both in `server.R` and `UI.R`.

Back to our example, imagine that the dataset that is being used changes after a certain time, and rows with certain species are added and removed. In this case, it would be more appropriate that the options in the species selector defined in `UI.R` are not hard coded but are defined dynamically based upon the `Species` variable in the dataset, as shown in *Example 4 – using global.R*.

Running a Shiny web application

In order to run a Shiny web application, it is important to consider that `UI.R`, `server.R`, and, if needed, `global.R` must be placed in the same folder. If an HTML document is used, a folder named www must be created in the application folder to hold the HTML document. Additionally, it must be named `index.html`.

There are three basic ways to run the applications. They are as follows:

- `runApp()`: This opens a browser and executes the application locally. It receives a string representing a directory as an argument. If no argument is provided, `runApp()` defaults to the working directory.

- `runGist()`/`runGitHub()`: This works exactly as `runApp()`, but instead of looking for the files locally, it connects to a gist or a GitHub repository, downloads the full application in a temporary file, and displays it in a web browser. This is explained in more detail in *Chapter 10, Sharing Applications*.

- URL: The web application is accessible to anyone that has the URL where it is located. In this case, it is not necessary for the application users to have R or RStudio on their computers. In order to have this, a server with `rstudio-server` and `shiny-server` installed is needed. Although the configuration of a public application is more complex than running it locally, it is definitely the most useful one as it enables access to almost any public application as only a web browser is needed. We will see more on this in *Chapter 10, Sharing Applications*.

An overview of simple examples

The Shiny package includes several examples. The `runExample()` command, with no arguments passed, displays the available examples as follows:

```
> runExample()
Valid examples are "01_hello", "02_text", "03_reactivity", "04_mpg",
"05_sliders", "06_tabsets", "07_widgets", "08_html", "09_upload", "10_
download", "11_timer"
```

To see the examples running, the name of the example must be passed as shown here:

```
> runExample("01_hello")
```

The examples are displayed in a separate window that includes the application and both `server.R` and `UI.R`, which generate them. The scripts are very well described so that it is easy to understand what each piece of code does:

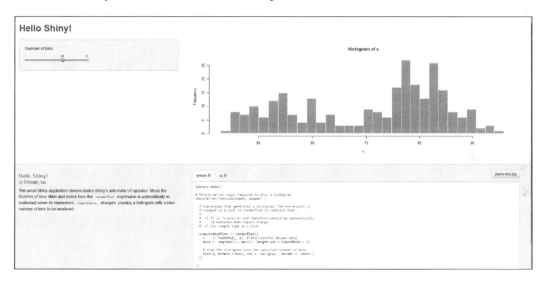

Some additional examples will be found in the following sections. The scripts for this application are available at Packt Publishing's website, where you can download all the examples in this book. To run it you have to either execute runApp("folder path"), pointing at the application's directory or, in the newest versions of RStudio, the program enables a button in the Shiny-related scripts to easily run the application.

```
server.R ×    UI.R ×                                               Run App
1   library(shiny)
2
3   #initialization of server.R
4   shinyServer function(input, output) {
5
6       #Plot generation
7       output$plot <- renderPlot({
8           plot(1/1:input$number)
9       })
10
11  })

11:3    (Top Level)                                                R Script
```

Example 1 – a general example of how render-like functions work

This first example consists of a very basic application where a number is passed, and a plot with the 1/x series, where x are the numbers between 1 and the passed number, is displayed. The following is the code for UI.R:

```
library(shiny)

# Starting line
shinyUI(fluidPage(

  # Application title
  titlePanel("Example 1"),

  sidebarLayout(

  # Sidebar with a numeric input
    sidebarPanel(
      numericInput("number",
                   "Insert a number:",
```

```
                      value = 30,
                      min = 1,
                      max = 50)
        ),


    #The plot created in server.R is displayed
      mainPanel(
        plotOutput("plot")
      )
    )
))
```

The following is the code for the `server.R` file:

```
library(shiny)

#Starting line of server.R
shinyServer(function(input, output) {

    #Plot generation
    output$plot <- renderPlot({
      plot(1/1:input$number)
    })


})
```

Keeping in mind the preceding diagram (in the *An introduction to server.R and UI.R* section), the logic applied to this example would be as follows:

1. The user inserts a number, and the number is stored in `input$number`. All the functions that draw widgets to pass inputs in `UI.R` have id as their first argument. Basically, they generate a JavaScript form with the id passed. They can be accessed afterwards by `input$(id)`.

2. The input is passed to `server.R`.

3. Due to its reactivity nature, `renderPlot()` in `server.R` is re-executed whenever a change in an input occurs.

4. The object created by `renderPlot()` is saved within the output list with the `output$(object_name)` form. This special object naming is necessary to be able to display the output in `UI.R`. Of course, when using render functions, output elements must match the type of the object that is being created. For example, returning a text in `renderPlot()` will not display any result in the application.

5. As there is a `plotOutput()` statement that calls the object generated in step 4, the Shiny framework passes that corresponding output to the browser.

6. Due to the specifications in `UI.R`, the object generated in step 4 is displayed. It is important to keep in mind that the displaying function (in this case, `plotOutput()`) must be compatible with the object that has to be displayed, that is, if the output object is of the plot type, it can only be called successfully by `plotOutput()`. If another function is selected, probably outputs that are not desired or no output will be displayed.

Usually, reactive objects are enclosed by both parentheses and braces. The braces in R denote an expression. An expression is basically a piece of code where even objects can be created. In this case, the objects created are only accessible inside the function they are in (in this case, `renderPlot()`). Back to the example, `renderPlot()` could also be written as follows:

```
renderPlot({
   numbers.to.plot <- 1/1:input$number
   plot(numbers.to.plot)
})
```

The `numbers.to.plot` object in this case is not accessible outside this call of `renderPlot()`. Although in this example the use of an intermediate object is absolutely trivial, it can be very useful if more complex scripts are required.

Example 2 – using reactive objects

As it was previously explained, R provides the possibility of creating intermediate reactive objects that can be used by other reactive functions, including those that effectively produce outputs. This is how `UI.R` looks like for the second situation explained in the *The concept of reactivity* section:

```
library(shiny)

# Starting line
shinyUI(fluidPage(

   # Application title
   titlePanel("Example 2"),

   # Sidebar with a numeric input
      textInput("text",
      "Insert a text:",
      value = "The cat is brown"),
```

```
#The plot created in server.R is displayed
    textOutput("text.words"),
    textOutput("text.longest")
  )
)
```

The following is the `server.R` file:

```
library(shiny)

#initialization of server.R
shinyServer(function(input, output) {

    #Plot generation
  output$text.words <- renderText({
  words <- unlist(strsplit(input$text, split = " "))
    paste0("This phrase has ",length(words)," words in total")

  })

  output$text.longest <- renderText({
    words <- unlist(strsplit(input$text, split = " "))
    word.chars <- nchar(words)
    max.len <- max(word.chars)
    longest.word <- words[which.max(word.chars)]

    paste0(longest.word, " is the longest word and has ",max.len,"
characters")

  })

})
```

As it can be seen, the `unlist(strsplit(input$text, split = " "))` expression is repeated. In this case, as there is not much processing required, an execution time difference cannot be practically appreciated. However, when it comes to larger amounts of data, doing the same process twice can be a real waste of resources. In order to avoid this, a reactive object can be created, which will then be used by both the `render()` functions. In this case, `server.R` would be as follows:

```
library(shiny)

#initialization of server.R
shinyServer(function(input, output) {
```

```
words <- reactive(unlist(strsplit(input$text, split = " ")))

#Plot generation
output$text.words <- renderText(
  paste0("This phrase has ",length(words())," words in total")

)

output$text.longest <- renderText({
  word.chars <- nchar(words())
  max.len <- max(word.chars)
  longest.word <- words()[which.max(word.chars)]

  paste0(longest.word, " is the longest word and has ",max.len,"
characters")

})

})
```

The repeated structure is called only once in a separate reactive expression and stored in the `iris.sset` object. As it is actually a function, the call of this object shall be done with the inclusion of parentheses. In this case, the subsetting is done only once and then used in both the render functions.

Example 3 – Loading data outside reactive context

This example is based on the iris dataset. It basically displays a summary of the variables based on the species selected. For this case, it is wise to call the dataset prior to launching the application, and this can be done by loading the data before the initialization of the Shiny server in the `server.R` script. `UI.R` and would look as follows:

```
library(shiny)

  # Starting line
shinyUI(fluidPage(

  # Application title
  titlePanel("Example 3"),

  sidebarLayout(

  # Sidebar
```

```
    sidebarPanel(
      #Species selection
      selectInput("species","Select a species:",
                    c("setosa","versicolor", "virginica"))),


    mainPanel(
      #The summary table created in server.R is displayed
      tableOutput("table")

    )
  )
))
```

The following would be `server.R`:

```
library(shiny)

data(iris)

#initialization of server.R
shinyServer(function(input, output) {

  #Table generation where the summary is displayed
  output$table <- renderTable(
    summary(subset(iris, Species == input$species)[,-5])
  )

})
```

 The fifth column of this dataset corresponds to the `Species` object. It has been taken out because, firstly, it is the subsetting condition (the nonselected species will have a frequency of 0) and secondly, the object type is not numeric (as the other variables are).

This is a good example of the usefulness of pre-loading processing. To produce an equivalent result without this, either `renderTable()` should include the call to the data or the data should be loaded in a reactive object. Both the options have a huge drawback that they imply inserting the same data load in a reactive process, that is, the same action will be repeated with no difference whenever an input changes.

The example with the data call in `renderTable()` would be as follows:

```
output$table <- renderTable({
  data(iris)
  summary(subset(iris, Species == input$species)[,-5])
})
```

Example 4 – using global.R

Looking at the same previous example, instead of hard coding the options in the species input widget, they could be taken directly from the `Species` variable of the dataset. To do this, the dataset must be loaded prior to the application load using `global.R`. This is how the different files would look like:

`global.R` will be a one-command file where only the dataset is loaded:

`data(iris)`

The following is the code for `UI.R`. Notice that the input options of species are not hard coded any more but are defined as the levels of the `Species` variable in the `iris` dataset:

```
library(shiny)

    # Starting line
  shinyUI(pageWithSidebar(

    # Application title
    titlePanel("Example 4"),

    # Sidebar
    sidebarPanel(
      #Species selection
      selectInput("species","Select a species:",
                  levels(iris$Species))),

    #The plot created in server.R is displayed
    mainPanel(
      #Table display
      tableOutput("table"),
      #Plot display
      plotOutput("plot")
    )
  )
  )
```

Finally, `server.R` differs from the previous example only in the fact that there is no need to load the data prior to initializing `shinyServer()`:

```
library(shiny)

#initialization of server.R
shinyServer(function(input, output) {

  iris.sset <- reactive({subset(iris, Species == input$species)[,-5]})

  #Table generation where the summary is displayed
  output$table <- renderTable({
    summary(iris.sset())
  })

  #Plot generation where the summary is displayed
  output$plot <- renderPlot({
    plot(iris.sset())
  })

})
```

The changes made in this example with respect to the previous one are only from the back end. From the end user's point of view, both applications will be identical.

Summary

In this chapter, the structure and main elements of Shiny's framework were covered. The main concepts underlying the Shiny package were also explained. Among these, reactivity is definitely the most important one.

Additionally, very simple examples were presented. These examples had the double function of providing an overview of how Shiny works and to see the main structures and concepts translated to a script.

Consequently, it is expected at this point that the user has a clear idea of what Shiny is, how it is built, and how it is coded. In the next chapter, more features and possibilities for the user's interface (`UI.R`) and the application's engine (`server.R`), in addition to some strategies for `global.R`, will be discussed.

5
Shiny in Depth – A Deep Dive into Shiny's World

By now, the reader should know what a Shiny web application is, how it is structured, and what its main underlying concepts are, reactivity being the most important one.

This chapter will be divided into the following two big topics:

- **UI.R and its different possibilities**: In UI.R, an intensive walkthrough of the different input and output types will be done. Some tips will be discussed in relation to the use of some of them.

- **A list of good practices for server.R and global.R**: As these applications run live, it becomes crucial to take execution times into account. In this regard, it is always important (especially when coding server.R and global.R) to find a way to produce the desired result to minimize execution times and coding, as this can give the application much better response times. This is the reason why there is a section dedicated to advice on how to structure and plan the application's development.

Additionally, a small section on Shiny's options configuration is also included.

UI.R

This section will cover the different parts of the interface with its corresponding functions. In short, we will look at the following:

- Structure, which will be divided into the following:
  - Pages
  - Layouts
  - Panels
  - Rows
  - Columns

- Inputs, which will be divided into the following:
  - Free inputs
  - Lists
  - Dates
  - Files
  - Buttons

The structure

Shiny provides some templates for web applications. They are general structures to organize the different elements within the interface, such as the position of the inputs, the position of the outputs, and so on.

Many of the elements related to structure are divided into fluid and fixed. The main difference is that fluid containers adjust the width of their elements to the browser's width while fixed is used with a user specified width.

Generally, elements in Shiny order themselves row-wise inside a structure, that is, one below the other. For example, the `structure1(elementA, elementB)` pseudocode will display `elementB` below `elementA` inside `structure1`. Although not recommended at all, the number of elements that can be placed one below the other is unlimited.

There are some builders, however, that order their elements column-wise, that is, one next to the other (for example, `sidebarLayout()`, which is explained in the following section). It is important to keep in mind that all structure-related functions have a width argument. Based on a 12 scale, this argument defines the width of the object in question with respect to the total width of the main structure that contains it.

So, for instance, if the container is 600 pixels wide, each width unit represents 50 (also 600/12) pixels. If the sum of the width of elements in the same row exceeds 12 pixels, the application will reorganize its elements and will not be able to display them in the same row. Finally, when the width argument is not specified, it is defaulted according to criteria that depend on the functions being used. It is important to keep in mind that decimal numbers are not accepted, i.e., you should use round numbers from 1 to 12.

You will find the most important builders related to structure divided by type in the following:

- **Page**: Page builders define the type of page that the application will be built on. In this sense, they are the first structure builders to be included, as they work as containers for the rest of the structures and the widgets. From a technical point of view, they create the structure of the HTML document that the application will be built on. The following is a list of page builders:

    ○ `fluidPage()`: This is the simplest main structure; a high-level function that creates a display adjusted to the browser's width. Along with `sidebarLayout()`, it is the simplest way to create a Shiny UI. In fact, the combination of `fluidPage()` and `sidebarLayout()` replaces `pageWithSidebar()`, which although deprecated, is still present in many examples on the Web.

    ○ `fixedPage()`: Unlike `fluidPage()`, `fixedPage()` creates a fixed-size application, independent of the browser's width. Unless it is explicitly required that the elements in HTML have a specific size, it is always advisable to use `fluidPage()` instead.

    ○ `bootstrapPage()`: This is the most basic type of page where only the JavaScript bootstrap library is loaded. It is worth remembering that this library is also called in the other page builders. For more information about bootstrap, visit `http://www.getbootstrap.com`.

    ○ `navbarPage()`: This creates a page with a navigation bar on top. It is used along with `tabPanel()`, which is explained in the following section of this chapter. An example of this can be found at `http://shiny.rstudio.com/gallery/navbar-example.html`.

- **Layout**: Layout builders generate empty structures with certain characteristics, where elements will be placed afterwards.

  - sidebarLayout():This creates a page with two main elements, a sidebar panel and a main panel. By default, their width is 4 and 8 pixels respectively. Both elements have their special builders, which are covered in the next section, sidebarPanel() and mainPanel(). Normally, the inputs will be placed in the Panel sidebar and the outputs in the main panel. Although this layout is suggested, it is a mere visual convention, so there is absolutely no restriction on placing inputs or outputs in any of them.

- **Rows and columns**: They are structures to include elements row or column-wise respectively.

  - fluidRow() and fixedRow(): Row functions are wrappers that display elements at the same height. In fact, the UI structure of a Shiny application is mainly thought of as consisting of rows with columns inside, at least for the simplest built-in functionalities. Lastly, it is advisable to use the function that corresponds to the main chosen structure.

While the fluid layout updates the width values whenever the browser's window changes, fixed layouts don't.

For fluid layouts, if the size of the window is changed (for instance, if it is maximized), then the width of the different tags update to fit the window's width.

In a fluid page, the width in pixels of the plot (inside the img tag) in a maximized window on a 1157 pixel-wide window is 1157.

On fixed layouts, on the contrary, this width update does not take place. As it appears in the manual, the total width default for fixedPage() is 940 pixels on a typical display, and 724 pixels or 1170 pixels on smaller and larger displays respectively.

As it can be seen in the preceding example, the input panel is enclosed in a div tag of the span4 class(that is, a panel of width 4, which means 4/12 from the total width) while the main panel is inside a span8 div. Naturally, these widths can be changed, with the only constrains that the sum of the widths within each row cannot exceed 12.

- **Panels**: Panels are delimited areas that serve a particular purpose. Normally, panels have either input or output elements:

  - inputPanel(): This is a panel to include inputs in one block. The function will place the different inputs from left to right and from top to bottom.

  - tabsetPanel(): This displays elements in tabs. It is particularly useful to display different outputs and group them in tabs by topic. A small demonstration based on the second example in the previous chapter is shown in the following section. The global.R script will not be included in this case because it remains exactly as it was.

  - absolutePanel(): This is a panel with a specified size and position. The position parameters will be taken as it is taken in CSS's absolute position. fixedPanel() is equivalent to this with the sole difference that it uses CSS's fixed position.

  - conditionalPanel(): This is a panel that is visible only if a certain condition is met. It can be used either to contain input or output elements. Two examples of different possible useful situations where this could be used and how it is done are shown in a later section.

  - tabPanel(): This is a tab structure that can be used inside navbarPage(), tabsetPanel(), or navlistPanel() to create tabs within the structure that contains it. By default, when a tab is not active, the outputs that are contained in it are not updated in the backend, even if the input changes.

  - sidebarPanel(): This is the sidebar's container for sidebarLayout(), that is, the sidebarPanel argument. By default, its width is 4 (out of 12, from Shiny's scale) and is aligned left.

  - mainPanel():This is the main container for sidebarLayout(), that is, the mainPanel argument. By default, its width is 4 (out of 12, from Shiny's scale) and is aligned left.

  - navlistPanel(): This is a very similar structure to navbarPage(), with the sole difference that instead of having the different tabs displayed on the top, they are displayed as links on the left-hand side within a box.

  - wellPanel(): This creates a basic Bootstrap's CSS well, that is, a colored (grey by default) container.

conditionalPanel() – Example 1

In the first example of the previous chapter, the application was used to send an error message when the input number was left blank:

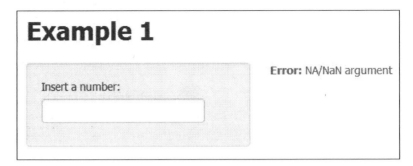

This error message is displayed because, as there is no input argument, the 1:input$number series in server.R returns NA, which, of course, results in an error while plotting. To avoid showing the user an error message, a conditionalPanel() builder can be included. In this case, the UI.R script would look as follows:

```
library(shiny)

# Starting line
shinyUI(fluidPage(

# Application title
titlePanel("Conditional Panel - Example 1"),

# Sidebar with a numeric input
# Sidebar
sidebarLayout(
  sidebarPanel(
    numericInput("number",
        "Insert a number:",
          value = 30,
          min = 1,
          max = 50)),


  #The plot created in server.R is displayed
    mainPanel(
      conditionalPanel(condition= "input.number > 0",
      plotOutput("plot"))
    )
  )
))
```

conditionalPanel() is included inside mainPanel(), and plotOutput() is passed inside conditionalPanel() after the condition. Every argument passed after condition= must be an element to be displayed if the condition is met. It is particularly important to take into account while using conditionalPanel() that the condition must be a string object representing a JavaScript statement.

In the case of inputs, they are called as input.(variable) in JavaScript. In this case, as the condition to be met is input.number > 0, whenever the condition is not met, (for example, when the input box is left empty) the output is not shown. In this case, the error message is not displayed:

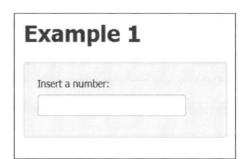

Dctacamp used another function for this

conditionalPanel() – Example 2

conditionalPanel() can also be used to selectively show inputs. Back to Example 1, if an optional parameter of color change is added, it would be coded as follows. In UI.R, a conditionalPanel() input is passed with the color change feature where the widget is inside conditionalPanel(), so it will consequently appear only if the condition passed to it is true (in this case, if the checkbox is ticked):

```
library(shiny)

# Starting line
shinyUI(fluidPage(

  # Application title
  titlePanel("Conditional Panel - Example 2"),

  # Sidebar with a numeric input
    # Sidebar
  sidebarLayout(
  sidebarPanel(
      numericInput("number",
                   "Insert a number:",
                   value = 30,
```

```
                min = 1,
                max = 50),
        #Checkbox to select color

        checkboxInput("selectcolor",label = "Change color"),

        #Conditional Panel. When the checkbox is ticked, it displays
        #the radio button options

        conditionalPanel("input.selectcolor == true",
          radioButtons("color", "Pick up the color:",
                    c("red", "blue", "green")))),


    #The plot created in server.R is displayed
      mainPanel(
        conditionalPanel(condition= "input.number > 0",
        plotOutput("plot"))
      )
    )
))
```

server.R would be as follows:

```
library(shiny)

#initialization of server.R
shinyServer(function(input, output) {

  #Plot generation
  output$plot <- renderPlot({
    if(input$selectcolor){
      plot(1/1:input$number, col=input$color)
    } else {
      plot(1/1:input$number)
    }
  })

})
```

In this case, whenever the checkbox is ticked, the radio buttons are displayed. As conditionalPanel() only makes parts of the application visible or invisible but does not have any influence on the input or output values that are contained in it, the color input variable (the one that receives the value from the radio buttons) will have a value, whatever status the checkbox has.

For this reason, the plot creation in server.R has to be slightly changed. Instead of directly plotting, it looks for the checkbox's input value (which is directly TRUE or FALSE as explained in the inputs section under checkboxInput()) and, if TRUE, it plots with the passed color. Otherwise, it is plotted with the default color (black).

Lastly, as the condition in condtionalPanel() is passed in a string of JavaScript code, true and false are written in lower case.

An example on the use of tabPanel() in tabsetPanel()

In the case of the iris dataset, a Tabset panel with two tabs is displayed in the output section where one panel is for the table and the other one is for the graphics.

In UI.R, tabsetPanel() only receives the tabPanel() objects. Inside these, the outputs are passed. The following is the UI.R code:

```
library(shiny)

# Starting line
shinyUI(fluidPage(

# Application title
  titlePanel("Tabset Example"),

  # Sidebar
  sidebarLayout(
    sidebarPanel(
      #Species selection
      selectInput("species","Select a species:",
      c("setosa", "versicolor", "virginica"))),

      #The plot created in server.R is displayed
      mainPanel(
        tabsetPanel(
          tabPanel("Summaries",tableOutput("table")),
          tabPanel("Graphics",plotOutput("plot"))
      ))

    )
  ))
```

In `server.R`, apart from creating the outputs, a reactive object was included, which is then used by both `renderTable()` and `renderPlot()`. As it was explained in the previous chapter, this is a very good practice when working with datasets, especially if the same dataset is used both times. Following is the code:

```
library(shiny)
data(iris)

#initialization of server.R
shinyServer(function(input, output) {

  sset <- reactive({subset(iris, Species == input$species)[,-5]})

  #Table generation where the summary is displayed
  output$table <- renderTable({
    summary(sset())
  })

  output$plot <- renderPlot({
    plot(sset())
  })

})
```

The following is the final outcome:

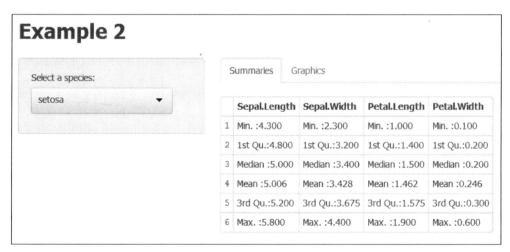

Inputs

The Shiny package provides a wide variety of input widgets to include in an application. It is also possible to create custom widgets. That is, however, out of the scope of this book, as an intermediate level in JavaScript is required.

The built-in Shiny widgets can be divided as follows:

- **Free input**: Fields to let the user insert a value freely
- **Lists**: User selects one or more items from a list
- **Dates**: Date/s selection from a calendar
- **Files**: User uploads a file
- **Buttons**: Buttons that trigger actions

Let's look at the most important functions in each of the sections.

Free inputs

Free inputs can mainly be divided in two big groups: numeric inputs and character inputs. They are as follows:

- `numericInput()`: This is a free field where the user can enter a number. Although Shiny provides the possibility of setting maximum and minimum values to this controller, it is important to keep in mind that, by default, the widget will only turn red, but the application will anyway execute with the entered number, unless the application itself performs a validation of the values entered on the server side, as it is explained in *Chapter 7, Advanced Functions in Shiny*.

- `textInput()`: This is a free field text where the user can write. Unfortunately, there is still no built-in option/feature to perform validations on free text inputs in the same way as in `numericInput()` for example, to validate whether the entered free text is an e-mail when an email is required.

- `sliderInput()`: A slider input is also a numeric input with the sole difference that instead of inserting a number in a free field, the input has to be determined by a slider. `sliderInput()` also has the advantage that it is limited to the range specified and that the interface itself does not allow the insertion of out of range values.

Lists

Although lists can be used for any other purpose, in most cases, lists are used to filter options. Conceptually, they can be subdivided into two big groups: unique and multiple selectors. Although for some of the list widgets to change from one type to another is as easy as setting multiple arguments to TRUE or FALSE, it is important to keep in mind that the object returned changes from a character to a character vector:

- `selectInput()`: This is the selection from a drop-down menu. Under the argument choices, the list of options can be passed as a character vector where the values displayed and the values stored in the corresponding input objects will be the same or as a character vector with names associated. In this case, the names will be displayed in the application but the value will be stored in the variable. Back to Example 2, if the name of the species should appear in capital letters, it would be as follows:

```
#Species selection
  selectInput("species","Select a species:",
  c(SETOSA= "setosa",
  VERSICOLOR="versicolor", VIRGINICA="virginica"))
```

 Vectors can have names assigned either by creating a vector and then assigning names with the names() function or directly during vector creation with c() and the = object structure name. It is not necessary that all elements contain names. In the second method, names can be passed quoted or unquoted. This applies for list() as well.

By default, `selectInput()` is a unique selection widget. In order to make it multiple, the `multiple` argument must be set to T.

- `checkboxGroupInput()`: This displays a list of checkboxes, with one checkbox per passed option. The object generated in the input list is exactly equivalent to `selectInput()` with `multiple = T`.

- `checkboxInput()`: This displays one single checkbox. Its outcome is TRUE or FALSE.

- `radioButtons()`: This displays options with radio buttons on its side. Functionally, it is exactly equivalent to `selectInput()` with `multiple = F`.

Dates

Shiny provides two built-in functions to select dates. Both of them have a very intuitive date-picker interface. The objects returned are date objects. However, in more advanced implementations, it is possible that in some cases, dates objects do not behave as expected:

- `dateInput()`: This is for date selection. The minimum and maximum values can be either a string in the yyyy-mm-dd format or a date object.

- `dateRangeInput()`: This is also for date selection. The minimum and maximum value can be either a string or a date object. Technically, it is equivalent to twice of `dateInput()`, with the sole difference that the function does not allow end values smaller than start values. The object returned in this case is an array of length two where the first element is the start and the second is the end.

Files

An interface for user file-upload can be included via `fileInput()`. It is highly recommended to add an action button (see the following) and an observation/isolation clause on the server side (*Chapter 7, Advanced Functions in Shiny*).

`fileInput()` creates a traditional file selection interface (that is, a button that, when hit, opens a window browser). The handling of this object will depend on the purpose of the application (whether it has to be turned into a data frame, to a list of lines, and so on).

Buttons

The following functions are the most important ones for buttons:

- `actionButton()`: This is a button that triggers an action. It is mostly used to prevent instant re-execution of code whenever an input changes. This functionality is most used in an isolation context. This topic is covered thoroughly in *Chapter 7, Advanced Functions in Shiny*.

- `submitButton()`: This delays the execution of any change in every input value until the button is hit. Although it might seem very similar to `actionButton()`, (in fact, there are many cases where both could be equivalent if properly used) they have a crucial difference: `submitButton()` changes all the input values at the same time, while `actionButton()` gives the possibility to trigger actions differently upon button hit. The difference can be seen very clearly when using a `conditionalPanel()` within an input area. You will find an example that illustrates the limitations of `submitButton()` in this situation in the following section.

submitButton() with conditionalPanel()

Back to the second example shown in the `conditionalPanel()` section (with the optional color selection), a slight change is made so that the execution of the changes in the input is carried out upon button hit.

In `UI.R`, only `submitButton()` is added as follows:

```
library(shiny)

# Starting line
shinyUI(fluidPage(

    # Application title
    titlePanel("Submit Button Example"),

    # Sidebar with a numeric input
      # Sidebar
    sidebarLayout(
    sidebarPanel(
        numericInput("number",
                    "Insert a number:",
                    value = 30,
                    min = 1,
                    max = 50),
        #Checkbox to select color
        checkboxInput("selectcolor",label = "Change color"),
        #Conditional Panel. When the checkbox is ticked, it displays
        #the radio button options
        conditionalPanel("input.selectcolor == true",
          radioButtons("color", "Pick up the color:",
                    c("red", "blue", "green"))),
        submitButton("Apply changes")),

    #The plot created in server.R is displayed
      mainPanel(
        conditionalPanel(condition= "input.number > 0",
        plotOutput("plot"))
      )
    )
  ))
```

`server.R` remains the same.

Although the only change with respect to the original example is the inclusion of the `submitButton()` widget, the application does not work as expected. Firstly, when the checkbox is checked, the radio buttons are not displayed. They will only display after the submit button is hit:

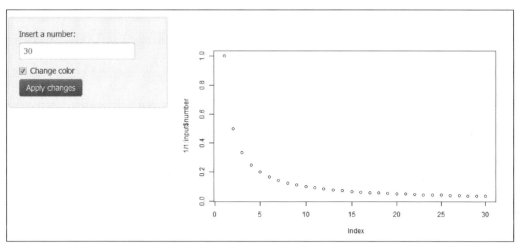

No change after the box is checked.

After this, the window will appear. At this moment, the user can click on any of the options, but the window will only change color once the button is hit again. However, when unchecking the box, the same problem appears; the radio buttons are still visible when they should be hidden.

This behavior is explained by the fact that `submitButton()` changes all the inputs at the same time upon button hit. So, not only will the color change depend on the button hit but also the checkbox value, which decides the visibility and invisibility of the radio buttons.

The solution to this would be the use of `actionButton()` instead. However, as this also requires the use of `isolate()`, which is a topic that will be covered in *Chapter 7, Advanced Functions in Shiny*, this same example will be taken up at that stage where its use will be much clearer to the user.

- downloadButton(): The name of this widget is clearly self-explanatory. This functionality is always used along with downloadHandler() in server.R. downloadHandler() is a function that serves exclusively to download data.

downloadButton() - an example

The following is a small applied example with the `iris` dataset.

Here's what `UI.R` should look like:

```r
library(shiny)

# Starting line
shinyUI(fluidPage(

  # Application title
  titlePanel("Example 2"),

  # Sidebar
  sidebarLayout(
  sidebarPanel(
    #Species selection
    selectInput("species","Select a species:",
      c("setosa", "versicolor", "virginica")),
      downloadButton("download", "Download Data")),

    #The plot created in server.R is displayed
    mainPanel(
      textOutput("report")
    )

  )
))
```

Here's what `server.R` should look like:

```r
library(shiny)

data(iris)

#initialization of server.R
shinyServer(function(input, output) {

  sset <- reactive(subset(iris, Species == input$species))

  #Text to output
  output$report <- renderText(
    paste0("The filtered dataset contains ",nrow(sset()), " rows")
  )

  #Download Handler
```

```
output$download <- downloadHandler(
    filename=paste0("Data_",input$species,"_",Sys.Date(),".csv"),
    content= function(file){
        write.csv(sset(),file, row.names=F)}
    )


})
```

The downloaded object has the name of the button that calls it. This means that in the flow of input/outputs, `downloadButton()` takes the object created by `downloadHandler()` and triggers the download.

`downloadHandler()` is a very special function that has a fixed structure that is unusual to traditional R coding under the argument content. Unlike normal CSV writing, Shiny writes the output to a temporary file and then constructs the file that will be downloaded. How this function works internally is very complex. However, respecting the structure as shown previously (`content = function(file){...}`), the application performs the data download with no problem.

While running these examples, it is important to keep in mind that the data download button does not work properly when running it on window (**Run in Window** option from the **Run App** button menu in RStudio). To do so, select **Run External** instead, and the application will be opened in a new tab on the active browser's session on newer versions of RStudio. In older ones, hit the **Run App** button and, once the window pops up, select **Open in Browser**:

Optimal usage of server.R and global.R

Unlike UI.R, the core of the code in `server.R` and `global.R` does not normally differ significantly from normal R code. The mean calculations, statistical functions, and so on are obtained exactly in the same way within a Shiny application as in any other script.

However, in the context where code gets re-executed constantly, like in the Shiny applications, and where eventually a multi-concurrence of users can occur, performance becomes a key factor to avoid collapses.

For example, if the whole application is based on one data source, there is no point in loading it more than once. So, in this case, if the data load code is within a reactive expression in server.R, the data will be loaded unnecessarily again whenever an input value changes, whereas it could have been loaded just once when the application was loaded.

Here are some tips to optimize your code and considerably reduce your execution time:

- **Run once whatever is used by more than one process**: In the reactive example shown in this chapter under the tabsetPanel section, for example, it was very clear that both renderPlot() and renderTable() used the same data source. However, this is not always so easy to identify. Before coding, it is always advisable to have an overview of the whole process, especially of what data is needed for each of the outputs. With this in mind, common processes can be identified and consequently run only once and stored in a reactive object.

- **Preload anything that can be preloaded**: As it happens with all the examples shown that load the iris dataset, it is always advisable to preload and preprocess everything that can be preloaded and preprocessed in global.R. In order to do this successfully, the programmer needs to have a clear idea of which elements in the application change and which don't.

  Those that don't change must be handled either in global.R or in server.R before the shinyServer() call so that the application only re-executes what is definitely necessary to re-execute. From a more general perspective, this is related to a clear understanding of the main concept underlying the Shiny applications, that is, reactivity. A clear idea of what is reactive and what is not will lead to successful preprocessing and preloading of whatever can be preloaded.

- **Build useful functions**: Building functions is a very good programming practice in general. Firstly, it reduces the amount of code written, and secondly, it spares massive eventual code modifications. For instance, if you need to do a change in a process that is not specified in a function, the change will have to be done in every place this process appears. Except for extremely exceptional cases, function declarations do not depend on reactive contexts, so it is also advisable when working with Shiny applications to declare all the functions either in global.R or in server.R before the shinyServer() call.

This list of good practices is valid for every code writing, not only in R but also in almost every programming language. But when it comes to web applications, where the response must be almost immediate, the execution times make the difference between a fair and an excellent job. Normally, web application users will be looking for fast answers to work in real time, so if the application cannot deliver the sought insights in time, it is simply not worth it.

Shiny options

In R, under `options()`, some settings regarding the use of R in general can be seen, for example, the number of digits printed for a number. These options can be modified by typing options (`option_name = value`), for example:

```
options(digits = 15)
```

Shiny has several options that are exclusive to the library. Almost all of them are defaulted to NULL. However, they can be changed in the same way as any other R option. Probably, the most important ones among them are `shiny.trace` and `shiny.error`. For `shiny.trace`, if TRUE, all of the messages sent between the R server and the web browser client will be printed on the console. This is useful for debugging (http://shiny.rstudio.com/reference/shiny/latest/shiny-options.html). For `shiny.error`, this can be a function that is called when an error occurs. For example, the option (`shiny.error=recover`) will result in the debugger prompt when an error occurs. The full list can be seen at http://shiny.rstudio.com/reference/shiny/latest/shiny-options.html.

Summary

After this chapter, the reader should have an overview of the different possibilities that a Shiny application can provide. Additionally, this chapter has provided some guidelines to optimize performance with a clear code that is easy to understand and maintain. Of course, the complexity of the applications will also depend on the programmer's R skills in general, independently from Shiny.

In the next chapter, we will look at some of the different graphical options that R provides, focusing on the `graphics` package (the most elemental package to produce graphics that comes with the base installation), `googleVis`, which is a package to create Google chart-like visualizations, and `ggplot2`, which is probably the most popular graphical package in R. Naturally, it will also be explained how to include these graphics in a Shiny web application.

6
Using R's Visualization Alternatives in Shiny

Normally, graphics are the central elements of data visualization as they are an intuitive and clear technique to display results, especially on a computer. In this chapter, you will learn about the different graphical procedures in R and how to integrate them in your Shiny applications.

By now, you must have acquired a clear notion of how to structure a Shiny web application and the different types of outputs that can be used. The purpose of this chapter is to complement this with a series of techniques to display data in a graphical way. In this way, unlike other software including commercial ones, R provides you with the possibility of displaying graphics (and any information in general) practically without restriction.

The importance of this goes far beyond a technical question. In alignment with GNU philosophy, no technical restriction implies no restriction in communication, which finally means "free" as in "free speech".

This chapter is particularly focused on the following three packages:

- `graphics`: The default package for graphics in R. Normally, this is installed along with R-core, so there is no need of a special installation.

- `googleVis`: This is a package to generate visualizations as in Google charts. For more information, visit `https://developers.google.com/chart/`.

- `ggplot2`: This is probably the most popular graphical package in R. Its main advantage is its flexibility. There's a book on this by Packt Publishing titled *ggplot2 Essentials, Donato Teutonico* (`https://www.packtpub.com/big-data-and-business-intelligence/ggplot2-essentials`).

The graphics package

As it was mentioned before, `graphics` is the most basic graphical package in R. As with any other package, it contains a wide variety of functions (all dedicated to graphics, of course) but `plot()` is the most important one. `plot()` is a special type of function called a generic function, which is a function that can receive inputs of different classes but produces different outputs according to the class of the input.

This can be simply appreciated by plotting the different variables of the `iris` dataset:

Variable type	Plot
If a character or factor vector is passed (such as `Species` from the `iris` dataset), a bar graph is returned: `plot(iris$Species)`	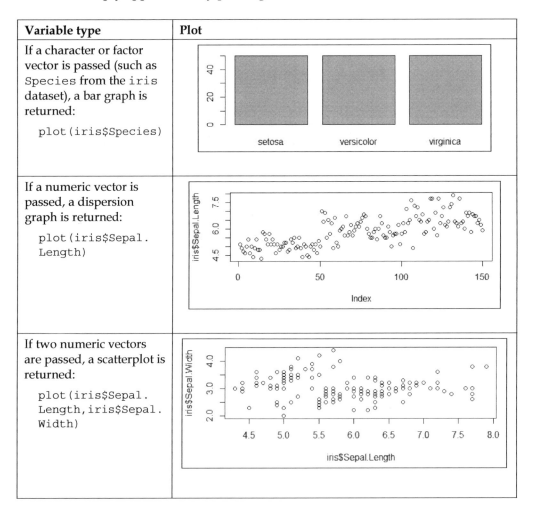

If a numeric vector is passed, a dispersion graph is returned:
 	
    `plot(iris$Sepal.`
    `Length)`	

If two numeric vectors are passed, a scatterplot is returned:
 	
    `plot(iris$Sepal.`
    `Length,iris$Sepal.`
    `Width)`	

Variable type	Plot
If a numeric data frame or matrix is passed, a multiple scatterplot is created: `plot(iris)`	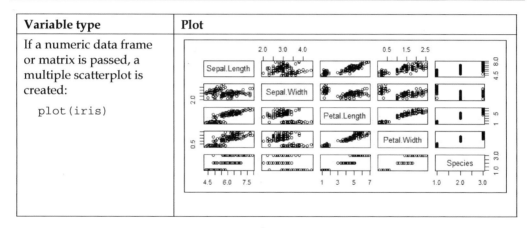

As you might have already realized, `Species` has been converted to a discrete numeric variable. This occurs whenever the data frame passed is a mix of numeric and categorical variables. In these cases, `plot()` transforms factors to numbers.

Multiple other examples could be passed with, naturally, multiple different outputs, such as dates, tables, linear model objects, clustering model objects, among many others.

To sum up, it is always a wise decision to see what `plot()` returns if the object created is passed to it.

Of course, the default `plot()` function is not the only one that is available in graphics. This package provides almost every traditional graphic as well. In the later sections, the following types of graphics will be covered:

- Barplot
- Histogram
- Boxplot
- Pie chart
- Points
- Lines

Barplot

`barplot()` has only one mandatory input, that is, either a numeric vector or a matrix. In the last case, the output is either stacked or placed one next to the other. This is controlled by the besides argument where FALSE returns the first case and TRUE the second.

When a matrix is passed, it has to be taken into account that the function will group by column. This is particularly important while plotting variables of datasets as they are organized by row. So, if two numeric variables of a dataset were selected, stored as matrix, and passed to barplot, then nonsense graphics would be returned as the bars would be stacked by case:

```
#This plot does not make sense
```

```
numeric.subset <- as.matrix(iris[1:5,1:2])
```

```
barplot(numeric.subset)
```

Instead, it is always advisable to use barplots with summarized data that is eventually grouped by another variable. In the case of the `iris` dataset, we can use barplots to plot the means of `Sepal.Length` and `Sepal.Width` (the first two variables in the `iris` dataset) by species.

The code would look as the following:

```
#This plot does make sense
```

```
#Generate aggregated data
```

```
aggregate.info <- aggregate(cbind(Sepal.Length, Sepal.Width) ~ Species,
data=iris, mean)
```

```
#Select the numeric variables of aggregate.info, convert it to matrix and
transpose it
```

```
aggregate.info.num <- t(as.matrix(aggregate.info[,c("Sepal.
Length","Sepal.Width")]))
```

```
#Add column names to new object, which will be each of the Species
```

```
colnames(aggregate.info.num) <- aggregate.info$Species
```

```
#Finally, plot
```

```
barplot(aggregate.info.num,beside=T)
```

This example shows that sometimes some graphics need prior data processing. This is the reason why data processing was covered earlier in this book. Although R in general has almost no restrictions in graphics, the suitable objects must be passed.

In the first line, the mean per species for both `Sepal.Width` and `Sepal.Length` is calculated by the `aggregate()` function and stored in the `aggregate.info` object. As barplot makes reasonable plots only with numeric matrices, it is necessary to select the corresponding variables and transform the object that is subset to a matrix. Additionally, as barplot works columnwise, the matrix is transposed. Finally, names are assigned to the columns of the transposed matrix, which will be the names of the species. This is useful to generate the labels and know to which species each bar belongs to.

In the `barplot()` function, the `beside` argument is passed as TRUE in order to put them one next to the other (rather than one above another). This is because stacked barplots suggest proportions.

Histograms

Histograms are a graphical method to display a continuous variable in segments. By default, R splits the variable by the `Sturges` method, which creates log2 from the size of the vector-passed and equally-wide bins.

However, this can be, of course, changed by the user by editing the breaks argument. One of the ways to do this is by passing a numeric vector, as shown in the following example:

```
hist(iris$Sepal.Length,breaks=c(4,6,8))
```

Apart from the plot, the `hist()` function returns a series of other outputs that might be useful. In order to see them, it would be best to assign the `hist()` output to an object and see what this contains:

```
> histogram.example <- hist(iris$Sepal.Length,breaks=c(4,6,50))
> names(histogram.example)
[1] "breaks" "counts" "density" "mids" "xname" "equidist"
```

Boxplots

Boxplots are very popular graphics among data scientists and statisticians. They are very useful as they give complete information about the distribution of the vector in question. Boxplots have two types of mandatory inputs: a numeric vector or a formula where the first variable is continuous, and a character or factor.

In the first case, only one boxplot will be returned while in the second one, a boxplot for each of the different values of the factor or character variable will be displayed. The following is a small example of this:

```
boxplot(Sepal.Length ~ Species, data=iris)
```

The output is as follows:

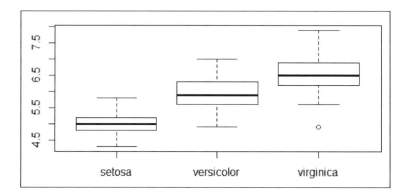

Pie charts

Although not considered for good data visualization, pie charts are very popular among non-expert public (that is, anyone who does not work specifically on data). This is not recommended, mainly because it is much more difficult to perceive differences in size of circular objects than of linear ones. For this reason, data visualization specialists do not advise the use of pie charts. However, as they are widely requested, it can be a necessary tool to have in the toolbox.

The function to draw a pie chart is simply pie(). Its main argument is a numeric vector, indicating quantities. If the elements of this vector have been named, then the chart will display these names. Otherwise, the labels argument can be specified, which is a character vector whose length is equal to the numeric vector passed:

```
> pie(table(iris$Species))
```

In this example, a named numeric vector is generated by the table() function, so pie() takes these values and labels to do the plot.

Points

points() is a function that draws points on an already existing plot. This is useful, for example, to draw two plots in one window or to add different sequences. The following is an example:

```
data(iris)
plot(iris$Sepal.Length)
points(iris$Petal.Length, col="red")
```

The output is as follows:

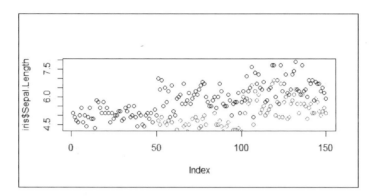

Lines

lines() is equivalent to points(), but instead of drawing points for each value, a line is drawn that connects the values in the sequence:

```
data(iris)
plot(iris$Sepal.Length)
lines(iris$Petal.Length, pch = 18, col="red")
```

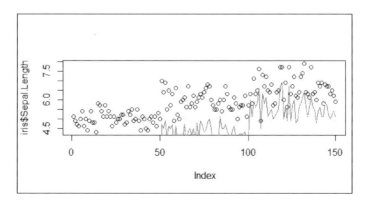

Plotting options

So far in the examples presented, the display of the plots has been just the default one. Of course, there are multiple possibilities of customizing this. For the purpose of extension, only the following listed ones will be covered:

- `col`: This is a string vector that defines the color. It can be written either as the color name (red, blue, and so on) or by its hexadecimal code. If the `col` argument has a vector shorter than the number of elements to plot, it will be recycled as explained in *Chapter 2*, *First Steps towards Programming in R*.

- `pch`: This argument defines the shape of the points plotted. The different options are numerically coded. For a complete reference, visit `http://www. endmemo.com/program/R/pchsymbols.php`.

Consequently, `pch` receives a numeric vector in which each number corresponds to one symbol according to the preceding image. This is similar to `col`, where the vector is recycled if needed:

- `main`: This is the title of the plot.
- `xlab`: This is the label of the horizontal axis.
- `ylab`: This is the label of the vertical axis.
- `xlim`: This specifies the lower and upper limit of the horizontal axis. A numeric vector of a 2 length must be passed to this argument. Here the first value indicates the lower limit, and the second value indicates the upper one.
- `ylim`: This is identical to `xlim` but for the vertical axis.
- `cex`: As stated in the R help, *A numerical value giving the amount by which plotting text and symbols should be magnified relative to the default* (`https:// stat.ethz.ch/R-manual/R-devel/library/graphics/html/par.html`). Although the explanation might seem complex, it is just a numeric value to control the relative size of the elements inside the plot.

Legends

As in `lines()` and `points()`, `legend()` is a function that needs to be called after the plot creation. `legend()` contains numerous arguments and most of them are optional.

The only mandatory arguments in `legend()` are x and `legend`, that is, the position and the texts that are passed to the legend. It is important to keep in mind that if y is not passed and a value is passed in x, this will be considered as a value in the vertical axis and the position with regard to the horizontal axis will be 1. If both the values (x and y) were specified, then the first will be the position in the horizontal axis and the second will be the position in the vertical axis.

The following two examples illustrate this difference. In the first one, as only one value is passed, this is interpreted as the value in the y axis. The height is specified by the vertical axis range, that is, the box's top of the legend will be drawn at the specified height. In the second one, two values are passed. In this case, the first value sets the position of the box's left-hand side while the second one determines the position of the top line of the box:

```
> plot(iris$Sepal.Length)
> legend(7.5,c("aaa","bbb"))
```

The legend on the top-left corner is as follows:

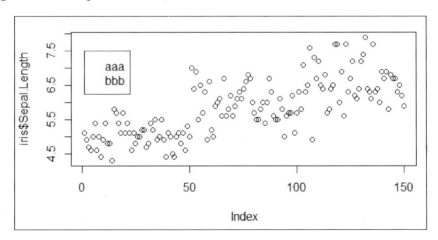

The legend on the bottom-right corner is as follows:

```
> plot(iris$Sepal.Length)
> legend(120,5.5,c("aaa","bbb"))
```

The output will be this:

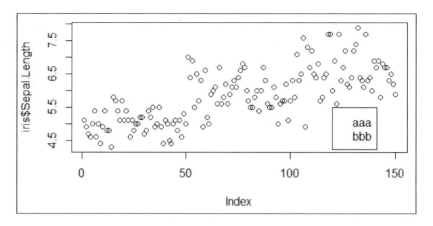

As it will be observed, most of the time using only the default arguments to generate a legend is not enough; legends are intended to give useful information to the reader to interpret the plot. The clearest example could be when we want to plot two series. Back to the `iris` example, if we would like to do a scatterplot of `Sepal.Length` and `Petal.Length` by `Species`, we would need to differentiate the series by species in some way.

The easiest method would be by color. In this case, for example, a legend would be needed to clarify to which series each color belongs. Although this task is very easy to fulfill in classical commercial software, in R, it is a bit more complicated. Of course, in this case, we would need to specify inside the legend what color each species belongs to.

In the following example, three series have been plotted. As it was explained before, `col` could be a character vector, so a new variable is added to the `iris` dataset. Using `switch()` along with `sapply()`, a color is assigned to every observation according to its species. After this, the plot is drawn by passing `iris$color` in the `col` argument.

Finally, the legend is added. In this example, its values (mainly, the legends and the colors) are passed as static strings. Of course, this code could be written in other ways to avoid, for example, by passing hardcoded `legend` and `col`:

```
data(iris)

iris$color <- sapply(iris$Species, function(x) switch(as.character(x),
    setosa = "red",
    versicolor = "green",
    virginica = "blue"))
```

```
plot(iris$Sepal.Length,iris$Petal.Length, col= iris$color, pch = 16)

legend(7.2,3,legend=c("setosa","versicolor","virginica"), pch=16, col=
c("red","green","blue"),cex=0.7)
```

This should be the output:

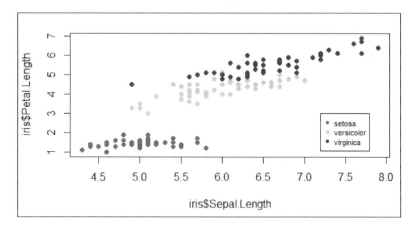

Plotting a fully customized plot with the graphics package

So far, we have seen the most important features of the graphics package and how to use its different options. To conclude, the following code adds custom labels and titles to the previous example:

```
data(iris)

iris$color <- sapply(iris$Species, function(x) switch(as.character(x),
setosa = "red",
versicolor = "green",
virginica = "blue"))

plot(iris$Sepal.Length,iris$Petal.Length, col= iris$color, pch =
16,main="Sepal Length/Petal Length dispersion graph",
xlab ="Sepal Length", ylab="Petal Length",cex=0.8, ylim=c(0,8))

legend(7.2,3,legend=c("setosa","versicolor","virginica"), pch=16, col=
c("red","green","blue"),cex=0.7)
```

This is the output:

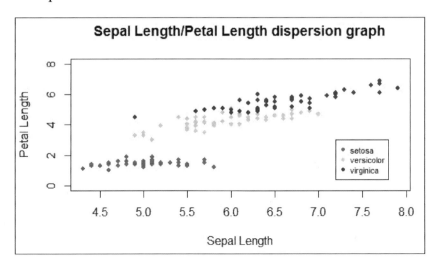

In this example, compared to the previous example, the vertical axis has been slightly extended on both the limits by specifying ylim, the dots have been made smaller (setting cex to 0.8), the axes labels have been changed (the xlab and ylab arguments) and a title has been added (main argument).

Including a plot in a Shiny application

When we include graphics inside a Shiny application, all the elements that are seen can be handled within a reactive context. Taking the same previous example, in the following code, you will see how to use reactivity inside graphical parameters.

In this case, a fixed color is assigned to every species, so the color assignment can be done outside the reactive context. In this case, we will be doing it inside global.R because the inputs in UI.R are going to be defined as the levels of iris$Species, as it was explained in *Chapter 4, Shiny Structure – Reactivity Concepts*:

```
global.R# Load Data
data(iris)

#Assign color by Species
iris$color <- sapply(iris$Species, function(x) switch(as.character(x),
setosa = "red",
versicolor = "green",
virginica = "blue"))
```

UI.R has two types of inputs; firstly, the species (within `checkboxGroupInput`) and secondly, the variables in the horizontal and vertical axes respectively. For the purpose of simplicity, the first part has been hardcoded. However, it could have been rewritten similar to the solution implemented for `selectInput()` where the variable names from the `iris` object were directly taken:

```
library(shiny)

# Starting line
shinyUI(fluidPage(

    # Application title
    titlePanel("Reactiveparameters in the application"),

    # Sidebar
    sidebarLayout(
    sidebarPanel(
      #Species selection
      checkboxGroupInput("species","Select the species to plot:",
        levels(iris$Species),
        selected= levels(iris$Species)),
        selectInput("xvar","Select the variable on the horizontal
axis",names(iris)[1:4]),
        selectInput("yvar","Select the variable on the vertical
axis",names(iris)[1:4])),

      #The plot created in server.R is displayed
      mainPanel(
        plotOutput("custom.plot")
      )

    )
))
```

It is in `server.R`, however, where the most important processes are done in order to have a fully flexible graph that can adapt to any variable combination and can still plot graphs with identical layout:

```
library(shiny)

#initialization of server.R
shinyServer(function(input, output) {

  iris.sset <- reactive(subset(iris,Species %in% input$species))
```

```
      species.color <- reactive(unique(iris.sset()[,5:6]))

    #Plot generation
    output$custom.plot <- renderPlot({
      title <- paste0(input$xvar,"/",input$yvar," dispersion graph")
      plot(iris.sset()[[input$xvar]],iris.sset()[[input$yvar]], col=
        iris.sset()$color, pch = 16,main= title,
      xlab =input$xvar, ylab=input$yvar,cex=0.8)

      #Horizontal Position for legend

      min.x <- min(iris.sset()[[input$xvar]])
      max.x <- max(iris.sset()[[input$xvar]])

      x.diff <- max.x - min.x
      x.pos <- min.x + x.diff * 0.8

      #Vertical Position for legend

      min.y <- min(iris.sset()[[input$yvar]])
      max.y <- max(iris.sset()[[input$yvar]])

      y.diff <- max.y - min.y
      y.pos <- min.y + y.diff * 0.2

      #Legend creation

      legend(x.pos,y.pos,legend=species.color()[,1], pch=16,
    col=species.color()[,2],cex=0.7)

    })

  })
```

Firstly, two reactive objects are created: `iris.sset`, which is clearly a subset by species and secondly, a small `species.color` dataset, which is mainly a deduplicated combination of species and color and used in the legend.

After this, the plot is rendered. In this case, the title object is dynamically built by pasting the variable names to the rest of the title together. In the plotting title, the object is passed to the `main` argument.

In the `plot` call, the variables selected for the horizontal and vertical axes are called with a double bracket. The reason for this is that as `input$xvar` and `input$yvar` are character strings, so they cannot be used to access the corresponding selected variables by writing something as `iris.sset()$input$var` or anything similar to this.

> As it was explained in *Chapter 2, First Steps towards Programming in R*, data frames are special types of lists. As lists, their objects can be accessed not only by the $ operator but also by index number or character string within double brackets. Sometimes both are equivalent but in this case, using the $ operator would have implied excessive complex coding.

For the positions of the horizontal and vertical axes, the range of the variable is calculated and after this, these positions are defined as the minimum value for the variable along with the range multiplied by a coefficient. As we want the legend near the bottom right corner, the coefficient in the horizontal axis is `0.8` (nearer to `1` than to `0`) and `0.2` on the vertical axis (nearer to `0` than to `1`). If the positions were hardcoded, the legend would move according to the selected variables because the axes would change whenever another variable is selected.

For the legend, the `species.color()` subset generated before is called where `legend` takes the first column of values and `col` takes the second one. Although this could have been coded differently, this solution guarantees that the color and species in the legend match correctly, independent of how the data is internally organized.

You may have realized at this stage that even with R's most basic graphical package, the possibilities of creating fully customized graphics within a Shiny application are endless.

A walk around the googleVis package

`googleVis` is a package in R that mainly interfaces R and Google Chart's API. This means that you can create Google charts within R via high-level functions. This has the great advantage of not needing to make service calls and parse the objects to generate the charts. Unlike traditional plotting in R, Google charts are displayed in a browser. In fact, their plot creation functions do not display a plot directly but generate an HTML code.

When working under R but not in a Shiny application, a `plot()` call with the HTML object as argument automatically opens a browser with the corresponding plot. The following is an example of this:

```
data(iris)

iris.table <- aggregate(Petal.Length ~ Species, data=iris, FUN="mean")

column.chart <- gvisColumnChart(iris.table,"Species","Petal.Length")
plot(column.chart)
```

As it was said previously, `gvisColumnChart()` does not generate a plot by itself but it generates a list with an HTML code that will generate the corresponding plot afterwards. This can be seen, if required, by typing the object name where the output was stored (in this case, `column.chart`) or by directly calling the function without storing it anywhere. This will display the generated list that contains the HTML code in the console.

From this small example, the advantages and disadvantages of this package can be already appreciated: the main advantage is that this enables us to create very attractive graphics (with tooltips and other types of in-graphic interactions) with very little effort. However, this has the drawback that the possibilities of customization are limited and in comparison to native R plotting options it is harder to code. Nevertheless, if what you need to display can be done within Google charts, the easiest and nicest way to do it will be probably in R.

googleVis in R

The `googleVis` functions tend to have unusual argument syntaxes. This relies on the fact that although most of the passed arguments and functionalities of Google charts have been adapted to R's coding style, there are still some parameters that need to be defined in an unusual way for R, especially when some layouts need to be different from the default.

Another unusual fact of the functions in `googleVis` is that they always receive a data frame. These data frames already must have the data ready to plot, as Google charts will only ask for the variables needed to do the plots from within the passed data frame. This relies on the fact that all these functions only transform the data frame to a JSON data object but perform no calculations unlike, for example, boxplots in the graphics package (in which the whole vector can be directly passed and R calculates the different values needed to do the plots).

Options parameter for the googleVis() functions

Almost every function in `googleVis` provides the possibility of changing some of the default layouts. In R, they can be changed by passing the desired value in the corresponding argument inside `options`. Unfortunately, the full documentation of the different options that can be edited is not available in R's package documentation.

However, they can be found at `https://developers.google.com/chart/interactive/docs/gallery`. All the options that appear in each of the functions can be edited in the way described. Some of the following examples illustrate how to do this.

An overview of some functions

As it happened with the previous graphics package, only some of the graphical possibilities will be covered in depth in this section. However, the package covered here provides a very good demo that can be run by typing the following:

```
demo(googleVis)
```

This statement triggers commented examples where the user can clearly appreciate what each function does and how it must be constructed. Anyway, for further questions, the documentation can be found at `http://cran.r-project.org/web/packages/googleVis/googleVis.pdf`.

These are the topics that will be covered within this section. They were chosen mainly due to their novelty. As it can be seen in the demo, `googleVis` provides all kinds of graphics but these are probably either unusual or different from traditional plotting options:

- Candlesticks
- Geolocalized visualizations
- Treemaps
- Motion charts

Candlesticks

Candlesticks are graphics packages designed for financial analysis to describe the behavior of a variable within a period of time. Originally, they were created to describe the behavior of stocks per day. Although, they look very similar to boxplots, candlesticks should not be confused with these as they represent completely different things.

In candlesticks, only four values from the series that they represent are displayed: the first one, the last one, the highest one, and the lowest one. The graph mainly consists of a rectangle whose height is the difference between the first and the last value. Of course, the lowest value between the first and the last value will represent the lower side of the rectangle while the highest value will represent the upper side.

The fill color of the rectangle will be different according to whether the first value is greater or smaller than the last value. Lastly, from the rectangle's top and bottom, two lines will be drawn until the lowest or highest value respectively.

The `googleVis` function that creates the HTML to do the candlestick charts receives a data frame and a string representing the name of the variable for each of the values needed to draw a candlestick chart (that is, low, high, open, and close). The categorical variable (that could be, for example, a date) goes under `xvar`. `gvisCandlestickChart()` will plot one candlestick per variable.

The following example shows an artificially created dataset that matches some conditions, for example, the low value is in fact the lowest one for each series, and then each variable is passed to its corresponding argument in `gvisCandlestickChart()`:

```
library(googleVis)
```

```
#Artificial dataset generation
```

```
example.data <- data.frame(year = 2005:2014, open = runif(10,0,100),
close = runif(10,0,100))
```

```
example.data$low <- apply(example.data[,2:3],1, function(x) min(x) -
runif(1,0,10))
```

```
example.data$high <- apply(example.data[,2:3],1, function(x) max(x) +
runif(1,0,10))
```

```
#Plotting
```

```
candlestick.chart <- gvisCandlestickChart(example.data, xvar = "year",
low="low",open="open",
```

```
close="close",high="high")
```

```
plot(candlestick.chart)
```

Geolocalized visualizations

Although there are other possibilities to display geolocalized visualizations, using `googleVis` is definitely the best one as Google charts is perfectly integrated to Google Maps to provide, in the end, very simple ways to display visualizations with maps and georeferenced data.

There are several different possibilities to plot geolocalized data in R, but they can be divided in two big groups: the ones that use `latlong` values, and the ones that refer to a geographical space by name (for example, a country name). Most of the functions that create visualizations based on geolocalized data accept both the alternatives as `locationvar`. Two examples using each of these are given in the following.

In the first one, an artificial data frame with approximate latlong values inside the USA is plotted. Here, region is set to US inside the options argument. The default for this argument is `world` (that is, display of the whole world):

```
library(googleVis)
#Artificial Dataset generation


latitudes <- runif(10,27,49)
longitudes <- runif(10,-125,-72)
values <- runif(10,0,100)


us.dataset <- data.frame(lat=latitudes,long=longitudes,val=values)


#Generate a latlong variable as expected in 'locationvar'


us.dataset$latlong <- paste(us.dataset$lat,us.dataset$long,sep=":")


#Map HTML creation


us.map <- gvisGeoChart(us.dataset, locationvar="latlong",sizevar="val",
options = list(region="US"))


#Plotting


plot(us.map)
```

Alternatively, different codes or names representing geographical regions can be used. In the following example, an artificial dataset for Brazil, Argentina, Peru, and Paraguay is built. After this, the same function as before is plotted but with some differences. Apart from changing the region, `displayMode` was set to `regions`. This causes instead of dots the whole surface of the country to be painted with the corresponding color:

```
#Artificial Dataset Generation

countries <- c("BR","AR","PE","PY")
value1 <- runif(4,0,10)
value2 <- round(runif(4,0,100))

sa.dataset <- data.frame(countries=countries,val1=value1,val2=value2)

#Plot of the Map. '005' is the region code for South America

southamerica.map <- gvisGeoChart(sa.dataset, locationvar="countries",size
var="val1",
hovervar="val2",
options = list(region="005",displayMode="regions"))

#Plotting

plot(southamerica.map)
```

Treemaps

Treemaps are very useful visualizations for hierarchies, that is, subelements that belong to a greater element. It displays the relationship between three dimensions: the hierarchy, the colors, and the size.

They are used in multiple different areas, such as computer science (for instance, to display directories and subdirectories), economy (a very good example of this is available at the MIT's Observatory of Economic Complexity, http://atlas.media. mit.edu/explore/tree_map/), and news (http://newsmap.jp/) among others.

gvisTreemap() is the function to create treemaps in googleVis. In the following code, the structure of this can be clearly seen. Firstly, idvar, the variable which indicates the name of the elements, is expected. In this case, this variable will be the regions variable. Each row must also have another row on which it depends or belongs to. This must be specified in another column and passed to the function in the parentvar argument.

As you can see from the following code, the root node, that is, the node that does not belong to another node, has an NA value under this column. gvisTreemap() only accepts one root node. The size variable determines the size of each of the squares. This is done, however, by comparing only the elements of the same node, for example, Asia, America, and Europe, or South America and North America. The values of Asia and South America neither the values of Japan and Brazil are compared. It's not necessary that the sum of the child nodes is equal to the parent node:

```
library(googleVis)

#Generate random data with dependencies

regions <- c("World","America","Europe","Asia","South America",
"North America","Western Europe","Eastern Europe", "Middle East",
"Far East", "Argentina","Brazil","USA","Canada", "Germany",
"France","Hungary","Russia","Israel","Saudi Arabia","China","Japan")

dependency <- c(NA,"World","World","World","America","America","Europ
e","Europe",
"Asia","Asia","South America","South America","North America",
"North America", "Western Europe", "Western Europe",
"Eastern Europe", "Eastern Europe", "Middle East", "Middle East",
"Far East", "Far East")

size <- runif(22,1,100)
color <- runif(22,1,100)

frame <- data.
frame(regions=regions,dependency=dependency,size=size,color=color)

#Plot treemap

treemap <- gvisTreeMap(frame, "regions","dependency","size","color")

plot(treemap)
```

Left-clicking on a square shows one level down (left-clicking on Asia displays Middle East and Far East) while right-clicking shows one level up.

Motion chart

Originally developed by Hans Rosling in GapMinder and now offered by Google under the name of motion chart, this is a visualization whose main advantage relies on the amount of variables it can display at the same time without compromising visual clarity.

In a very general way, this describes the evolution of a series of variables over time. It consists mainly of bubbles whose positions depend on their values for the variables represented on the X and Y axes and whose color and size depict the value of the other two variables. These last two parameters are optional; in case they are not used, the bubbles will be of the same size/color.

A very impressing example of a problem described with motion charts is given by Rosling himself in this video: https://www.youtube.com/watch?v=jbkSRLYSojo.

For the following example, an additional WDI package was installed. WDI is a package that retrieves data from the World Bank API. As this type of visualization requires a temporal variable, WDI data is very easy to display in this kind of graphs. For this example, some arbitrary indicators and countries were taken. In this case, a variable was assigned to every option, even to size and color:

```
#Install WDI to obtain data from the World Bank API and call the
library(gooeglVis)

install.packages("WDI")
library(WDI)

# Load some data

indicators <- c("BM.KLT.DINV.GD.ZS","BG.GSR.NFSV.GD.ZS","EN.ATM.CO2E.
PP.GD","NY.GDP.MKTP.CD")
countries <- c("AR","BR","DE","US","CA","FR","GB","CN","RU","JP")

frame <- WDI(country = countries, indicator = indicators, start =
2005, end=2013)
```

```
#Change indicator names just to make it easier to understand

names(frame)[4:7] <- paste0("indicator",1:4)

#Graph HTML Creation

motionchart <- gvisMotionChart(data = frame, idvar = "iso2c", timevar
= "year", xvar = "indicator1", yvar = "indicator2", sizevar =
"indicator3", colorvar = "indicator4")

#Plotting

plot(motionchart)
```

This visualization is similar to a small dashboard, as it provides us with the possibility of changing the variables of the different indicators (each of them has a small drop-down menu with all the available variables in the dataset) or even changing the type of visualization shown by clicking on one of the icons in the top-right corner.

googleVis in Shiny

googleVis in Shiny has two particular characteristics that are worth mentioning: firstly, it has its own reactive function, which only works for googleVis visualizations. This function is renderGvis(). In the next example of a Shiny web application done entirely with googleVis, it is shown clearly how this works.

Another particular thing about googleVis is that, instead of plotOutput(), it uses HTMLOutput() in UI.R. This makes absolute sense if we consider that the output of all the googleVis functions are mainly HTML code

A small example of googleVis in Shiny

Taking the World Bank example in the motion chart, in the following, you will find a Shiny application done entirely with the googleVis visualizations that you can reproduce as any other example, simply by creating the same files that appear here.

 Due to some reasons that definitely exceed the scope of this book, the following example works properly only on a separate browser. This means that after running it, please select **Run External** in newer versions of RStudio, or click on **Open in Browser** and test this from the browser window in older ones.

In `global.R`, the WDI library is used, which is mainly an interface to connect to the World Bank API and where data from different indicators can be retrieved by year and country. In this script, firstly, all indicators are retrieved with `WDIsearch()` and some indicators are chosen (the election was arbitrary). After this, the data for these indicators for an arbitrary list of countries between 2005 and 2013 is retrieved.

Finally, an indicator vector and a country vector is created. These vectors are named just to illustrate how a named vector works in `UI.R`. However, this is not necessary. Have a look at the following code snippet for `global.R`:

```
#Call WDI library

library(WDI)
library(reshape2)
library(googleVis)

#Load all indicators

all.indicators <- as.data.frame(WDIsearch())

#Take 6 indicators

used.indicators <- all.indicators[c(1:3,12,14,15),]

#Retrieve Data from indicators

countries <- c("AR","BR","DE","US","CA","FR","GB","CN","RU","JP")


frame <- WDI(country = countries, indicator = as.character(used.
indicators[,1])
             , start = 2005, end=2013)

#Create indicator's vector

indicators.vector <- as.character(used.indicators[,1])
names(indicators.vector) <- as.character(used.indicators[,2])

#Create countries' vector

countries.vector <- unique(frame$iso2c)
names(countries.vector) <- unique(frame$country)
```

In UI.R, the input options are defined by the data retrieved in global.R. As it was explained, UI.R uses the named character vectors in checkboxGroupInput() and selectInput(). If a named vector is passed, the names are displayed in the applications frontend while the variable adopts the value from the selected element. With respect to sliderInput(), the minimum and maximum values are directly taken from the dataset created in global.R.

This strategy of passing the values by reference, instead of hardcoding them, is much more flexible. In case any change of countries or indicators is done in global.R, UI.R will keep working.

In the output section, a tabset with two tabs is displayed: one for the intensity map, and the second one for the motion chart. The following code is for UI.R:

```
library(shiny)

# Starting line
shinyUI(fluidPage(

  # Application title
  titlePanel("World Bank Dashboard with GoogleVis"),

  # Sidebar
  sidebarLayout(
  sidebarPanel(
      #Country selection
      checkboxGroupInput("countries","Select the countries:",
              countries.vector,
              selected=countries.vector),

      #Years selection
      sliderInput("years","Select the year range",min(frame$year),max
(frame$year),
              value = c(min(frame$year),max(frame$year))),
      #Map variable selection
      selectInput("map.var","Select the variable to plot in the
map",indicators.vector)),

  #The plot created in server.R is displayed
    mainPanel(
      #htmlOutput("MotionChart")
      tabsetPanel(
```

```
        tabPanel("Map Chart",htmlOutput("Map")),
        tabPanel("Motion Chart",htmlOutput("MotionChart"))
    )
  )


    )
  ))
```

In `server.R`, subsets of the data are first created according to the filters applied. After this, each of the functions that create their visualization work differently according to their needs. In order to create the map, a sum aggregation by country code is performed for every variable. This is needed because the original dataset is split by years; in this case, one value per item (that is, country) is needed.

After this, the selected variable in the drop-down menu (`selectInput()`) is selected to be the intensity variable (passed in the `sizevar` argument). This piece of code can be optimized as some variables are needlessly aggregated in the aggregation phase (basically, all the variables that will not be used).

 Unfortunately, there is no link to provide here. The optimization relies mainly on the way it is coded. Basically, the aggregation expression can be written by dynamically taking only the variable needed, but this would have required an explanation of expression objects, which is definitely a more advanced stage of R.

The dataset for motion chart graphics on the contrary does not need any modifications in order to make it work. This is the reason why the chart creation function is called directly with the corresponding variables passed to it. The following is the code for `server.R`:

```
library(shiny)

#initialization of server.R
shinyServer(function(input, output) {

  frame.sset <- reactive({subset(frame,iso2c %in% input$countries &
    year >= input$years[1] &
    year <= input$years[2])})

  #Table generation where the summary is displayed
  output$Map <- renderGvis({
    aggregated.frame <- aggregate(.~iso2c + country,frame.sset()[,-3],
sum)
    map <- gvisGeoChart(aggregated.frame, locationvar="iso2c",sizevar=
input$map.var,
```

```
      hovervar="country",
      options = list(region="world",displayMode="regions"))
    return(map)
    })

  output$MotionChart <- renderGvis({
    mchart <- gvisMotionChart(frame.sset(), "country","year")
    return(mchart)
  })

})
```

ggplot2 – first steps

ggplot2 (an acronym for **Grammar of Graphics plot**) is the most popular graphical package in R. This relies mainly on the fact that almost anything can be drawn with it. This huge flexibility, however, implies more complexity while drawing.

The underlying concept of ggplot2 is an empty canvas. Instead of specifying the type of plot and the data to be visualized, the ggplot2 functions expect vectors that denote positions, widths, sizes, and so on. From its conceptual point of view, this is very similar to an HTML document; this is an empty space that is filled with different objects to which different characteristics are specified. The following example is the equivalent of plot(iris$Sepal.Length):

```
ggplot.graph <- ggplot(data=iris)                        y axis
ggplot.graph <- ggplot.graph + geom_point(aes(1:150,Sepal.Length))
                                                   X axis
plot(ggplot.graph)
```

This example is a typical ggplot code. As the reader might have already realized, its construction differs significantly from the other packages seen so far. In this section, the logic underlying ggplot2 will be explained and the functionality of the different elements in the following example will be clarified.

By this stage, it is only necessary for the reader to understand that when the points are specified with geom_point(aes(1:150, Sepal.Length)), the X and Y coordinates have to be specified. In this example, the position along the horizontal axis is defined as a vector from 1 to 150 (the number of cases in the iris dataset) while the position along the vertical axis is defined by the Sepal.Length vector.

ggplot's main logic – layers and aesthetics

Layers and aesthetics are two key elements within ggplot. There is no possibility of using this package in all its potential without a solid understanding of these two aspects.

Layers

The ggplot objects were previously described as empty canvases. This definition is, however, incomplete; the ggplot objects are empty canvases that are filled by layers. It is, in fact, the superposition of layers that makes ggplot so flexible. Let's examine the previous example again:

```
ggplot.graph <- ggplot(data=iris)
ggplot.graph <- ggplot.graph + geom_point(aes(1:150,Sepal.Length))

plot(ggplot.graph)
```

Firstly, a ggplot object is initialized. This is important to take into account that in order to create visualizations in ggplot2, a ggplot object must be created first. After this, layers can be added. In this example, only one layer consisting of points (the geom_point() function) is added to the object. The addition of layers to a ggplot object is mostly performed by the + operator (there are other options too, but they are rarely used).

At this stage, it is important to understand the difference between a ggplot object and a layer; the first one is the canvas and the second is the one with the elements displayed in it. So, their behaviors are different. The following points describe some of these behaviors, and consequently, what can and cannot be done with each of them:

- The addition can be performed only between the ggplot objects and the layer objects, that is, the following operations are not permitted:
  - ```
    ggplot() + ggplot()
    ```
  - ```
    geom_point() + geom_point()
    ```
- The layer objects cannot be plotted. That is, operations such as plot(geom_point(aes(1:150,1:10))) are not permitted.
- The addition of a ggplot object and a layer object is a ggplot object with a layer. This means that more than one layer can be added to the same ggplot object, or intermediate ggplot objects can be built with successive layers:

```
ggplot.graph0 <- ggplot(data=iris)
```

```
ggplot.graph1 <- ggplot.graph0 + geom_point(aes(1:50,Sepal.
Length[1:50],colour="red"))

ggplot.graph2 <- ggplot.graph1 + geom_point(aes(51:100,Sepal.
Length[51:100],colour="blue"))
```

```
plot(ggplot.graph2)
```

Aesthetics

Aesthetics in `ggplot2` is where the parameters of the elements to be displayed are specified, such as position, color, and size. The most commonly used function to build this is `aes()`, but in some cases, `aes_string()` or `aes_q()` might be more useful.

These functions can be called either in `ggplot()` or in any of the layers. It is important to consider that some of the arguments that can be passed to `aes()` might not be applied to the object passed. For example, specifying `linetype` in `aes()` for the `geom_point()` function does not have any effect. In the documentation, it is specified which aesthetics arguments are understood by each of them. However, it is important to take into account that these mistakes will not throw an error.

When adding layers, the parameters passed to `aes` are inherited, replaced, or overridden if they are not specified. This will depend on the addition type used. In the most common case (the + operator), the parameters specified in the layer will be overridden. However, this override is only valid in the layer specified. This means that if a new layer is added, it will not inherit the `aes` characteristics of the previous layer but of the ones from the `ggplot` object. Let's examine the following example:

```
library(googleVis)
```

```
ggplot.graph <- ggplot(data=iris)
```

```
ggplot.graph <- ggplot.graph + geom_point(aes(1:50,Sepal.
Length[1:50],colour="red"))
```

```
ggplot.graph <- ggplot.graph + geom_point(aes(51:100,Sepal.
Length[51:100]))
```

```
plot(ggplot.graph)
```

In this example, the `data` argument is defined in the `ggplot` call. As this is not overridden, every variable referred in the `ggplot` object is bound to the dataset specified. This is the reason why the y position is written simply as `Sepal.Length`. However, as the color in the second layer is not specified, the default (black) is taken, that is, the object does not inherit the color from the previous layer.

Some arguments can be passed both inside or outside aes(). In fact, the preceding example does not use the coloring attribute properly; the arguments passed to aes() are intended to have a meaning in the data. This is the reason why they are normally not a constant but a variable in the dataset. In fact, every aspect argument referring to some visual characteristic of the plot passed to aes() will be automatically included in the legend.

If the aesthetic change does not have any meaningful information regarding the data that is being displayed (for example, changing the color of the points in a geom_point() graph due to design), it is always better to pass it outside aes() as this will not create extra meaningless references.

Some graphical tools in ggplot2

In this section, only a few layers will be explained just to illustrate concrete examples of ggplot2. However, it is strongly advised to investigate more deeply about possibilities of ggplot2 if the reader wants to include these visualizations in their applications. In the later sections, the following functions will be covered:

- geom_point
- geom_line
- geom_bars

geom_point

geom_point() draws points whose positions are specified by the x and y arguments inside aes(). In the following example, the positions are defined by Sepal.Length and Sepal.Width. Additionally, color is specified by Species:

```
library(googleVis)

points.graph <- ggplot(data=iris)

points.graph <- points.graph + geom_point(aes(x=Sepal.Length,y=Sepal.Width, colour=Species))

plot(points.graph)
```

This is the expected outcome:

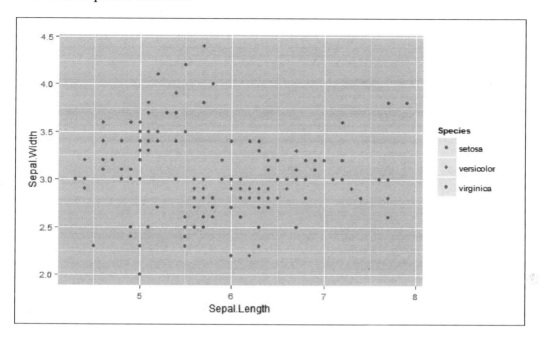

geom_line

`geom_line()` draws a continuous line that binds each subsequent coordinate pair given by x and y in `aes()`. If group is specified, then the lines are drawn by groups. In the preceding example, the x coordinate is defined by `Sepal.Length` while the y coordinate is given by `Sepal.Width`. As the grouping is already specified as `Species` in the `ggplot` call, three lines (one per group) are drawn. The color is also defined by `Species`:

```
library(googleVis)

line.graph <- ggplot(data=iris, aes(group=Species))

line.graph <- line.graph + geom_line(aes(x=Sepal.Length,y=Sepal.Width,
colour=Species))

plot(line.graph)
```

This is the expected outcome:

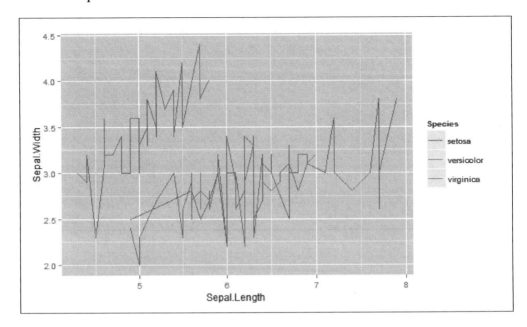

geom_bars

`geom_bars()` builds a layer consisting of bars. Its only mandatory argument in `aes()` is x. Unlike `geom_point()` or `geom_lines()`, the x argument of `geom_bars()` expects a factor (or a variable that can be coerced to be this). The function calculates the frequency per category and returns the corresponding bar plot. In the following example, a barplot is build for the `variable` class in the `mpg` dataset:

```
library(googleVis)
bar.graph <- ggplot(data=mpg)
bar.graph <- bar.graph + geom_bar(width=0.3, fill="red", aes(x=class))
plot(bar.graph)
```

This is the expected outcome:

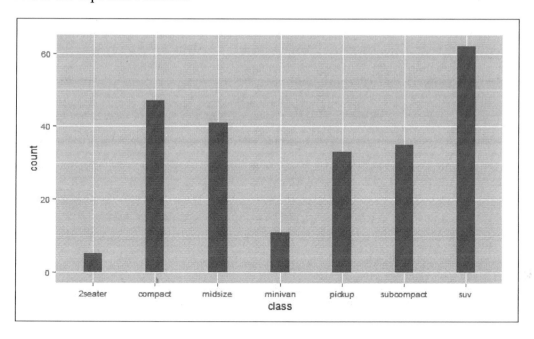

An applied example with multiple layers

One of the most interesting capabilities of `ggplot2` is the possibility of combining layers. In the following code, a very simple plot is created that consists of two layers, a `geom_point()` that draws all the points corresponding to the second anscombe series (the `x2` and `y2` variables respectively), and a line between the first and the last observation.

 The anscombe quartet is an artificial dataset originally conceived by Francis Anscombe where each x-y set has the same mean and variance for both variables, the same correlation coefficient, and the same regression equation. However, by plotting them, it becomes clear that they are all very different. In R, this is available by default as `iris`.

The data is sorted before so that the first and last observations match with the first and last values of x in the plot:

```
library(googleVis)
data(anscombe)
sorted.anscombe <- anscombe[order(anscombe$x2),]
anscombe.graph <- ggplot(data=sorted.anscombe)
anscombe.graph <- anscombe.graph + geom_point(colour =
"blue",aes(x=x2,y=y2))
anscombe.graph <- anscombe.graph + geom_segment(colour = "red",aes(x=x2[1
],xend=x2[nrow(anscombe)],
y=y2[1],yend=y2[nrow(anscombe)]))


plot(anscombe.graph)
```

This is the expected outcome:

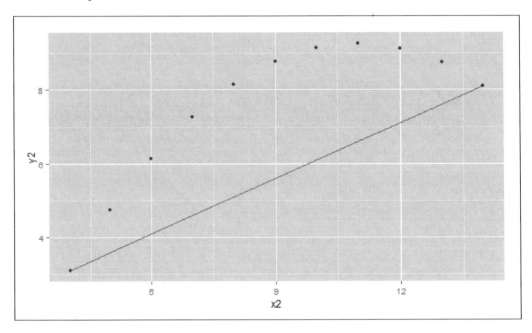

ggplot and Shiny

When integrating ggplot2 in Shiny, there is probably one main issue to consider: aes() accepts expressions (that is, unquoted variable names) as arguments but there is no widget in Shiny that can produce an input value of that class. For this reason, in most of the cases, it will be advisable to instead use aes_string(), which can receive character arguments.

The following server.R file is an equivalent in ggplot for the server.R file of the graphics Shiny example in the *Including a plot in a Shiny application* section. As ggplot already draws the legends and re-adjusts the scales automatically, the code ends up being much clearer than in the first case. As it was already explained, aes_string() is used instead of aes() because input$xvar and input$yvar are character values. ggtitle() is, as expected, a layer that adds a title to the ggplot.

By replacing server.R from the first example with the following code, an equivalent visualization will be obtained with the sole difference that the plot will have a ggplot look and feel:

```
library(shiny)

#initialization of server.R
shinyServer(function(input, output) {

  iris.sset <- reactive(subset(iris,Species %in% input$species))

  #Plot generation
  output$custom.plot <- renderPlot({
    iris.ggplot <- ggplot(data=iris.sset())
    iris.ggplot <- iris.ggplot + geom_point(aes_string(input$xvar,
input$yvar, colour="Species"))
    iris.ggplot <- iris.ggplot + ggtitle(paste0(input$xvar,"/",input$y
var," dispersion graph"))
    plot(iris.ggplot)

  })

})
```

Summary

This chapter is intended to be a mere introduction to the graphical capabilities of R and how they can be inserted into Shiny web applications. As it was already mentioned, good visualizations are the key to success with this kind of tool, and for this reason, it is always useful to master as many resources as possible. However, building good applications does not rely only on a technical fact (that is, being able to code it) but also on other soft skills that are related more to business understanding, generating impact, and so on. The last chapter of this book covers the development of an application with Shiny from scratch in a hypothetical real-world situation where some problems related to this communicational aspect of the application are presented and solved.

Next chapter goes back to Shiny package specifics again and will cover some advanced functions that will definitely broaden the horizons of your application's possibilities with just a few lines.

Advanced Functions in Shiny

7

At this stage, it is supposed that you already know how to code web applications in Shiny with certain complexity. In this chapter, three main topics will be covered that will help you to expand the possibilities of your applications a step further. They are mainly four functions that operate on the server side (that is, they are used in the `server.R` script):

- `validate()`: This validates the inputs passed according to some condition
- `isolate()`: This prevents the update of a piece of code given a change in a reactive value
- `observe()`: This provides a reactive context but generates no displayable output
- `reactiveValues()`: This creates a list object whose element can deal with reactive values
- **Input updates**: These are a group of functions that change one or more characteristics of a specific input (for example, `sliderInput` would require `updateSliderInput`).

The validate() function

The name of this function is definitely self-explanatory. In almost all the cases and except for extremely rare occasions, `validate()` is used along with `need()`, which is an easy wrapper that evaluates an expression in an extended way and produces an error message.

The expression evaluation performed by need() is extended with respect to normal condition evaluation in R, because it evaluates to False (and displays an error message) if the evaluation returns NA or the passed variable is empty. need() has two arguments for the error message: message and label. The first one is simply the text to be displayed and the second one is a character that can be used to be inserted dynamically into the error message. By default, message is paste(label, "must be provided"), so it expects the label argument. However, if message is passed, label is ignored. It is normally recommended to directly specify message.

Looking at *Example 1* again, this could be a good need() statement to include:

This displays if number ≤ 0

```
need(input$number > 0, "Provide a number greater than 0")
```

warning message

In this case, if no number or any number smaller than or equal to zero is passed, need() will pass to validate() a warning that the number provided is not valid. validate() supports multiple need() calls and displays the error messages of the need() calls whose expressions were evaluated as False.

validate() is used inside a render expression such as renderPlot() or renderText(). This prints an error message (which can be the concatenation of various error messages) and stops the execution of any output object that is rendered afterwards. As validate() basically prints an error message, it is always advisable to place it before the sentence that effectively produces the output (for example, plot() in renderPlot()). Although there might not be any obvious difference for the end user, placing validate() before the plot call will prevent the program from making the plot. If this is placed afterwards, the application will create the plot but will put the error message above instead.

Again, taking the first example provided in this book, the following code shows clearly how this function is used and the results it produces in server.R (UI.R remains exactly as the first example):

```
library(shiny)

#initialization of server.R
shinyServer(function(input, output) {

  #Plot generation
  output$plot <- renderPlot({
    validate(
      need(input$number > 0, "Provide a number greater than 0"),
      need(input$number < 100, "Provide a number smaller than 100"))
    plot(1/1:input$number)
```

easy to understand

```
    })


    })
```

You can see for yourself how the error messages are displayed. As it was explained previously, due to the evaluation mechanism of need() if no number is passed, both messages are displayed. This is a very good outcome in terms of usability purposes as it provides the end user all the necessary information of the input value expected for that field.

The isolate() function

[handwritten: Isolate piece of code; called only within a reactive context]

isolate() is a function that does exactly what is expected; it isolates a piece of code. In a Shiny reactive context, this means that it prevents the execution of a piece of code unless, of course, certain condition is met. The condition that isolate() takes in order to re-execute the piece of code is, however, not evaluated in the usual way (that is, in the way that returns TRUE or FALSE), it evaluates whether the object changes or not.

The object to evaluate the condition that is mostly used within isolate() is the action button. The actionButton() function, apart from drawing a button in the interface, creates an object, which is mainly a counter that whenever the button is hit, it increases its value by 1. It becomes clear then why isolate is used mainly with actionButton(); it is ideal to isolate a piece of code from the reactive context it is in until a button is hit.

Lastly, isolate() is a function that can be called only within a reactive context, that is, inside a render-like function (renderPlot(), for example), a reactive expression (reactive()), or within observe(), a function that is covered in this chapter.

In *Chapter 5, Shiny in Depth – A Deep Dive into Shiny's World*, we had explained a problem that appeared with the use of submitButton(). Basically, as the button executes all the input changes at the same time, there was no possibility of ticking the box to change the dot colors that displayed the colors menu, select the color, and then hit the button to produce the output. With actionButton() and isolate(), it can be specified which input variable changes should be delayed until the button is hit and which ones should be executed immediately.

In this case, the checkbox that made the colors visible should be executed immediately, while the rest of the inputs should change only on the button hit. UI.R changes only in the input widget that is passed and has both input Id and label:

```
library(shiny)

# Starting line
shinyUI(fluidPage(

    # Application title
    titlePanel("Submit Button Example"),

    # Sidebar with a numeric input
      # Sidebar
    sidebarLayout(
    sidebarPanel(
        numericInput("number",
                     "Insert a number:",
                     value = 30,
                     min = 1,
                     max = 50),
        #Checkbox to select color
        checkboxInput("selectcolor",label = "Change color"),
        #Conditional Panel. When the checkbox is ticked, it displays
        #the radio button options
        conditionalPanel("input.selectcolor == true",
           radioButtons("color", "Pick up the color:",
                        c("red", "blue", "green"))),
        actionButton("run","Apply changes")),

    #The plot created in server.R is displayed
      mainPanel(
        conditionalPanel(condition= "input.number > 0",
        plotOutput("plot"))
      )
    )
))
```

In the following code of server.R, the change of input$run is set to be the condition of the output's re-execution:

```
library(shiny)

#initialization of server.R
```

```
shinyServer(function(input, output) {

  #Plot generation
  output$plot <- renderPlot({

    #Isolation condition
    input$run

    isolate({

      if(input$selectcolor){
        plot(1/1:input$number, col=input$color)
      } else {
        plot(1/1:input$number)
      }

    })

  })

})
```

The value of `input$run` is a hit counter of `actionButton()`. For this reason, whenever the button is hit, the value of `input$run` changes and consequently, the code inside `isolate()` is executed.

Although from a usability point of view, it would not make much sense, the condition variable to be used along with `isolate()` can be anything. The following scripts, for example, create an application where the changes are done whenever the checkbox is ticked/unticked.

This is a standard frontend with a checkbox. The following is the code snippet for `UI.R`:

```
library(shiny)

# Starting line
shinyUI(fluidPage(

  # Application title
  titlePanel("Example 1"),

  # Sidebar with a numeric input
  # Sidebar
  sidebarLayout(
```

```
    sidebarPanel(
        numericInput("number",
        "Insert a number:",
        value = 30,
        min = 1,
        max = 50),

    #Checkbox
    checkboxInput("selector",label = "Checkbox")
    ),

    #The plot created in server.R is displayed
    mainPanel(
        plotOutput("plot"))
    )
))
```

In this case, the input$selector variable changes from TRUE to FALSE instead of being an incremental integer. However, the behavior of the isolate() clause is the same one. This is how server.R looks like:

```
library(shiny)

#initialization of server.R
shinyServer(function(input, output) {

    #Plot generation
    output$plot <- renderPlot({
        #Isolation condition
        input$selector

        isolate({
            plot(1/1:input$number)})
        })

})
```

In the preceding example, the plot is only updated if the user ticks/unticks the checkbox.

The observe() function

From the functions covered in this chapter, observe() is definitely the most difficult to understand. Going deeper into the preceding definition, observe() generates outputs from reactive values (inputs) that are not rendered in an application and cannot be used inside another reactive context (for example, renderPlot() or reactive()). As a consequence of this, this function will be rather used to generate a backend process that depends on reactive values.

observe() can be used, for example, to download data depending on reactive values on the server side, such as keeping track of the application's use in a text file, similar to a log. Another very common use of observe() is to update the arguments of an input widget based on reactive values. This will be covered in the last section of this chapter.

In the following example, the application keeps track of the numbers passed as input by saving them in a log. Inside observe(), the passed values (given that it is not NA) are stored in the values log.txt file. There is no need to create the file before calling the application, as it will automatically create it if it is not found by the application. Otherwise, as the append argument is set to T, the new values will be always appended to the file. The following is the code for server.R:

```
library(shiny)

#initialization of server.R
shinyServer(function(input, output) {

  #Plot generation
  output$plot <- renderPlot({
    plot(1/1:input$number)
  })

  observe({
    if(!is.na(input$number)){
    sink("values log.txt", append=T)
    cat(input$number)
    cat("\n")
    sink()}
  })

})
```

The reactiveValues() function

reactiveValues() creates a list of objects that can operate with reactive values but are not reactive values themselves. The main difference is that reactiveValues (unlike reactive objects) are not re-executed whenever an input value changes.

Due to this, reactive values are an optimal tool whenever certain register of previous inputs is needed. A good example of this could be counting the number of times an input value changes. In this case, a code is needed where the value of the counter depends on the input value change and on the counter's own previous value. As there is no possibility of operating with reactive values outside a reactive context, this should be inside a reactive context. In this case, as the result will not be displayed inside the application, the code will be inserted inside observe().

The first idea would be to place a counter inside observe(). With the first example, the code should look like this in server.R:

```
library(shiny)

#initialization of server.R
shinyServer(function(input, output) {

  observe({
    counter <- 0
    if(!is.na(input$number)){
      counter <- counter + 1
      cat(counter, sep ="\n")}
  })


  #Plot generation
  output$plot <- renderPlot({
    plot(1/1:input$number)
  })
})
```

The counter value would be normally stored frequently, but in this example, in order to make it easier to understand the idea of reactive values, the counter value will be just printed in the console. However, in this example, 1 is constantly printed. This is due to the fact that the observe clause is re-executed whenever the input changes. This means that the counter is reset whenever the value is changed. It is in these kinds of cases where a reactive value is needed, that is, an object that is created outside a reactive expression is updated depending on inputs but is not re-executed whenever an input changes.

Now that we know that we need a reactive value, a second approach in `server.R` would be something like this:

```
library(shiny)

#initialization of server.R
shinyServer(function(input, output) {

  reactiveval.list <- reactiveValues(counter = 0)


  observe({
    if(!is.na(input$number)){
      reactiveval.list$counter <- reactiveval.list$counter + 1
      cat(reactiveval.list$counter, sep ="\n")}
  })


    #Plot generation
    output$plot <- renderPlot({
    plot(1/1:input$number)
  })
})
```

> Run this code for a couple of seconds only as it can crash your computer.

In this case, numbers are printed endlessly and independently of a user's input. This is due to the fact that although the `reactiveval.list$counter` counter is inside an `observe()` clause, in this case, the update condition (the dependency) relies only on the fact that `input$number` is not NA. So, unless `input$number` is NA, the piece of code will be re-executed. The underlying problem here is that the code should be re-executed based upon two conditions: `input$number` is not NA and the value of `input$number` has changed.

For this reason it is necessary in this case to isolate the counter. The reactive value that will trigger the execution of the counter in this case will be, of course, `input$number`. Take a look at the following code for `server.R`:

```
library(shiny)

#initialization of server.R
shinyServer(function(input, output) {
```

```
reactiveval.list <- reactiveValues(counter = 0)

observe({

  input$number
  isolate({
     (!is.na(input$number)){
        reactiveval.list$counter <- reactiveval.list$counter + 1
        cat(reactiveval.list$counter, sep ="\n")}
  })
})


#Plot generation
output$plot <- renderPlot({
   plot(1/1:input$number)
})
})
```

As it can be seen in this example, the combination of the three methods introduced, isolate(), observe(), and reactiveValues(), is perfectly possible. In fact, this is sometimes the only way to develop certain functionalities in Shiny. For this reason, it is very important to have a clear understanding of how each of them works and what can be done with them. This is can be only achieved by using them.

Input updates

These functions are particularly useful when the options of an input are determined in some way by another input. For example, if a continent was one input and a country the other, the options of the latter would be restricted by the selection of the first.

In order to use input updates, the Shiny server needs to be initialized with an additional session argument. This means that the following should not be the starting line:

```
shinyServer(function(input, output){
```

Instead of the preceding code, this must be the starting line:

```
shinyServer(function(input, output,session){
```

Session is an optional parameter that can be included in the Shiny server function calls. This creates an object of the session class that keeps track of certain session information. For input updates, the session object is needed as it contains a function to communicate with the inputs (sendInputMessage) and consequently update it. However, there is no need to have a deep knowledge about session objects, as the high-level update functions can deal with them. For more information about this, visit Shiny's documentation at http://cran.r-project.org/web/packages/shiny/shiny.pdf.

The following scripts correspond to the example mentioned previously, where the countries' selections are determined by the continent and changed by updateSelectInput(). Then the selected countries are highlighted. The display is at the continent level.

Note that as the options for checkboxGroupInput() are directly determined, in this case, by updateCheckboxGroupInput() on the server.R side, its choices argument has just one empty value. This is required by the function, as the argument cannot be left empty. However, as the continent input variable always has a value assigned, the checkbox options are constantly updated (on the server side), and, for this reason, the widget always appears with its corresponding choices. To leave the choices argument with one empty value in UI.R is a decision that meets the need of this specific problem, but this does not mean that it is a rule whenever you use updateCheckboxGroupInput(). The following is a code for UI.R:

```
library(shiny)

# Starting line
shinyUI(fluidPage(

  # Application title
  titlePanel("Countries Update Example"),

  # Sidebar with a numeric input
  # Sidebar
  sidebarLayout(
    sidebarPanel(
      selectInput("continent", "Select the continent: ",
      c(Africa", "America", "Asia","Europe"),
      selected = "Africa"),
      checkboxGroupInput("country",
      "Select the countries:",choices = c(""))
    ),

    #The plot created in server.R is displayed
```

```
      mainPanel(
        htmlOutput("map"))
    )
  ))
```

It is in `server.R` where actually the different options are determined. Within `observe()`, the `continent.countries` object adopts the values corresponding to the continent input with a switch expression. You can learn more about switch expression in *Chapter 2, First Steps towards Programming in R*. It is important to consider that `update` functions will be called almost always inside an `observe` clause; creating an application with input updates coherent whenever one of the inputs is dependent on another. In this sense, as the update must evaluate a reactive input, it should be placed inside a reactive context, and as the update does not really generate an output (it just updates the arguments of an existing one), it must be included inside an observer.

The plotting is done with `geoChart` of `googleVis`. Inside the expression, firstly, an artificial dataset is generated in order to pass the data to `geoChart` in the exact way it is needed. For more information, see *Chapter 6, Using R's Visualization Alternatives in Shiny*. In this case, the dataset is directly generated inside the `renderGvis()` reactive expression instead of creating a reactive expression outside the plotting function. As there is no other process that uses this dataset, in this case, it is better to keep the expression inside the function. As it was already explained in *Chapter 6, Using R's Visualization Alternatives in Shiny*, `gvisGeoChart()` expects a code in its region argument, so the continent cannot be passed directly. For this reason, the continent code is determined by switch, stored in an object, and passed to the region argument:

```
library(shiny)
library(googleVis)

#initialization of server.R
shinyServer(function(input, output, session) {

  #Plot generation
  output$map <- renderGvis({

    validate(
      need(length(input$country) > 0, "Please select at least one
      country"))
    plot.dataset <- data.frame(countries = input$country, value=5)

    continent.code <- switch(input$continent,
      Africa = "002",
      America = "019",
      Asia = "142",
      Europe = "150")
```

```
        gvisGeoChart(plot.dataset, locationvar="countries",sizevar="val
ue",
        options = list(region=continent.code,displayMode="regions"))

    })


    observe({

        continent.countries <- switch(input$continent,
        Africa = c("Tunisia","Egypt","South Africa","Lybia"),
        America = c("Argentina","Brazil","Mexico","USA"),
        Asia = c("China","Japan","India","Indonesia"),
        Europe = c("France","Germany","Italy","Spain"))

        updateCheckboxGroupInput(session,"country",choices = continent.
countries)
    })
})
```

Note that when running the plot, if no country is selected, an error is thrown referring to the list in general (arguments imply differing number of rows: 0, 1). This is because the data frame created inside renderGvis() used by gvisGeoChart() cannot be generated, as the input$country argument is empty. Of course, it is not correct that the applications display these kinds of mistakes not correct, especially if they are going to be consumed by end users who do not have any technical experience in R as it gives them the impression that there is an error in the application.

In these cases, a validation can be used. As it has been explained previously, the error message in validation is custom and it can be used to provide the user with more information of what is still needed from them in order to display an output. In this case, for example, the message would be similar to Please select at least one country. This is how server.R would look like with this validation instance:

```
library(shiny)
library(googleVis)

#initialization of server.R
shinyServer(function(input, output,session) {

  #Plot generation
  output$map <- renderGvis({

    validate(
```

```
            need(length(input$country) > 0, "Please select at least one
country"))

        plot.dataset <- data.frame(countries = input$country, value=5)

        continent.code <- switch(input$continent,
            Africa = "002",
            America = "019",
            Asia = "142",
            Europe = "150")

        gvisGeoChart(plot.dataset, locationvar="countries",sizevar="val
ue",
        options = list(region=continent.code,displayMode="regions"))

    })


    observe({

      continent.countries <- switch(input$continent,
          Africa = c("Tunisia","Egypt","South Africa","Lybia"),
          America = c("Argentina","Brazil","Mexico","USA"),
          Asia = c("China","Japan","India","Indonesia"),
          Europe = c("France","Germany","Italy","Spain"))
          updateCheckboxGroupInput(session,"country",choices = continent.
countries)
      })

  })
```

However, not just the choices of an input can be updated. These input update
functions can operate on any of the arguments of the functions that they are
updating. In the following example for UI.R, consider the phrase of the second
input is updated according to the species selected:

```
library(shiny)

# Starting line
shinyUI(fluidPage(

  # Application title
  titlePanel("Iris"),

  # Sidebar
```

```
    sidebarLayout(
      sidebarPanel(
        #Species selection
        selectInput("variable","Select a variable:",
          setdiff(names(iris),"Species")),

        # Value input
        numericInput("value","",value=0,min = 0)
      ),

      #The plot created in server.R is displayed
      mainPanel(
        tableOutput("table")
      )

   )
))
```

This is how `server.R` looks when the `label` argument is changed based on the selection:

```
library(shiny)

#initialization of server.R
shinyServer(function(input, output,session) {

  observe({

    input.label <- paste0("Select the minimum value for
",input$variable,":")

    updateNumericInput(session,"value",label = input.label)
  })

  #Table generation where the summary is displayed
  output$table <- renderTable({
    subset(iris, get(input$variable) > input$value )})

})
```

The example is very simple; it just displays a subset of `iris` based on the variable selected and the minimum value passed. In `UI.R`, instead of manually adding all the variables in `selectInput()`, `setdiff()` is used, a function that excludes the values in the second argument from the first one. In `server.R`, the input's text is updated via a very simple dynamic text object with `paste0`. Finally, the `subset()` expression inside `renderTable()` uses `get(input$variable)` because `input$variable` is a string and the subset expects an expression. In other words, `get()` is telling subset, in this case, that the string must be treated as a variable from `iris`.

To sum up, from the `update` functions, the following must be clear:

- There is one corresponding update function for each input function.
- Update functions do not create reactive outputs, they just update the existing ones. So, if they depend on a reactive value in any way (which they will most surely do), they have to be called within an observer.

Summary

Advanced Shiny functions are definitely harder to understand, as they are conceptually different from everything seen so far in Shiny. However, they expand the application's possibilities enormously. This can be seen even in the example codes. Before this chapter, the examples were much simpler in terms of the application's functionalities since the reactivity process was also much simpler; whenever an input changes, the output is updated. Thanks to these functions, the reactivity process can be much more complex, the execution can be controlled, invisible processes can be triggered, and so on. Dealing with this complexity, far from being a problem, is a huge advantage.

The functions presented in this chapter belong, metaphorically speaking, to a second level of functions in terms of complexity. There are some other more advanced functions that provide more advanced possibilities. However, as this is an introductory book, these will not be covered here. If you are interested in more advanced functionalities of Shiny, we encourage you to do deeper research using the package's documentation, the specialized forums, and so on.

In the next chapter, we will focus on the relationship of Shiny and JavaScript and discover how to insert JavaScript code into Shiny's applications.

Shiny and HTML/JavaScript

8

As it was already explained in the introduction, Shiny has practically no boundaries. Apart from the built-in capabilities that the package provides, the developer can also code their own HTML document instead of the UI.R file.

This HTML document is as any other document of its kind and can include the same things (for example, CSS, jQuery, JavaScript, and so on). In fact, UI.R files are, as it was previously mentioned, a mere wrapper that generates an HTML document with JavaScript, CSS, and so on.

This chapter is focused on the inclusion of custom JavaScript or CSS code in a Shiny application. In this sense, it is important to consider that it is not a JavaScript or CSS tutorial, and not even an introduction; it simply illustrates the different ways of including a few pieces of code from the previously mentioned languages in Shiny. This chapter is divided into the following four sections:

- The www directory
- Creating UIs from plain HTML
- Using tags
- Relating HTML/JavaScript and server.R

The www directory

The www directory is the directory expected by a Shiny application to locally store the elements that will be rendered in the web browser and are not the output of the scripts. This includes images, HTML, .js files, and so on. This directory must be at the same level as UI.R and server.R, that is, on the application's main folder.

Back to the first example, if we would like to include an image of the R logo that is stored as Rlogo.jpg before the number input, the code will be as follows in UI.R:

```
library(shiny)

# Starting line
shinyUI(fluidPage(

  # Application title
  titlePanel("Example 1"),

  # Sidebar with a numeric input
  # Sidebar
  sidebarLayout(
  sidebarPanel(
    img(src="Rlogo.jpg"),
    numericInput("number",
      "Insert a number:",
      value = 30,
      min = 1,
      max = 50)),


    #The plot created in server.R is displayed
    mainPanel(
      plotOutput("plot")
    )
  )
))
```

This folder is the destination of the files generated in the following sections. For this reason, it is always necessary to keep in mind that if the application needs any external document, this should be included in this www folder.

Creating UIs from plain HTML

UIs from plain HTML, require firstly that the HTML file is stored in the www folder and secondly, that the file is named as index.html. Naturally, creating a whole interface in HTML without any of Shiny's UI functionality requires considerable experience in web programming. For this reason, in this section, we are going to reproduce *Example 1* only, but with an HTML file instead of an UI.R file.

In order to do this, create a copy of `Example 1` folder as follows:

1. Copy the following code and paste it in a text editor. You are strongly recommended to use text editors that support syntax highlighting. Probably, the best option is Notepad++, which is accessible from `https://notepad-plus-plus.org/`. Save the file as `index.html` in the `www` folder that will be created in step 2.

2. Inside the `new` folder, create the `www` folder:

```
<!DOCTYPE html>
<html>
<head>
  <meta http-equiv="Content-Type" content="text/html;
charset=utf-8"/>
  <script type="application/shiny-singletons"></script>
  <script type="application/html-dependencies">json2[2014.02.04];j
query[1.11.0];shiny[0.11.1];bootstrap[3.3.1]</script>
<script src="shared/json2-min.js"></script>
<script src="shared/jquery.min.js"></script>
<link href="shared/shiny.css" rel="stylesheet" />
<script src="shared/shiny.min.js"></script>
<meta name="viewport" content="width=device-width, initial-
scale=1" />
<link href="shared/bootstrap/css/bootstrap.min.css"
rel="stylesheet" />
<script src="shared/bootstrap/js/bootstrap.min.js"></script>
<script src="shared/bootstrap/shim/html5shiv.min.js"></script>
<script src="shared/bootstrap/shim/respond.min.js"></script>

  <title>Example 1</title>
</head>
<body>
  <div class="container-fluid">
    <h2>Example 1</h2>
    <div class="row">
      <div class="col-sm-4">
        <form class="well">
          <div class="form-group shiny-input-container">
            <label for="number">Insert a number:</label>
            <input id="number" type="number" class="form-control"
value="30" min="1" max="50"/>
          </div>
        </form>
      </div>
      <div class="col-sm-8">
```

```
        <div id="plot" class="shiny-plot-output" style="width:
100% ; height: 400px"></div>
      </div>
    </div>
  </div>
</body>
</html>
```

3. Delete the UI.R file.

4. Run the application by any of the methods mentioned here. You should see the same application as in *Example 1*.

This is intended to be a mere introduction of how the frontend in Shiny applications can be eventually fully customized by creating the HTML document. Although this might seem simple, creating an application's frontend in HTML is probably a task for experienced web developers.

At this point, there seems to be a complex dichotomy: whether we take Shiny's built-in user interfaces or we create a fully customized one by coding it in HTML from scratch. Fortunately, the Shiny package provides an intermediate solution with the tags object, which provides the possibility of customizing the frontend by adding only pieces of HTML, JavaScript, and so on inside UI.R, that is, without needing to create the whole HTML document from scratch. In the following section, it will be explained how to do this.

The use of tags in UI.R

tags is an object of type list that is automatically generated inside Shiny applications, which enables the insertion of HTML tags within a user interface generated in UI.R. This basically contains a list of functions that will transform the string argument to the content of the tag used, for example, see the following:

```
tags$pre("Text inside a pre tag")
```

This generates the following tag:

```
<pre>Text inside a pre tag</pre>
```

 The complete list of tags can be found at http://shiny.rstudio.com/articles/tag-glossary.html.

Attributes can be passed to any of the functions in tags by passing them as arguments, for example:

```
tags$pre(align="right","Text inside a pre tag")
```

This will be turned into the following HTML:

```
<pre align="right">Text inside a pre tag</pre>
```

In the following UI.R code, the previous piece of code is included. This generates a pre-tag with the text before the number insertion widget:

```
library(shiny)

# Starting line
shinyUI(fluidPage(

  # Application title
  titlePanel("Example 1"),

  # Sidebar with a numeric input
    # Sidebar
  sidebarLayout(
  sidebarPanel(
    tags$pre(align="right","Text inside a pre tag"),
      numericInput("number",
                   "Insert a number:",
                   value = 30,
                   min = 1,
                   max = 50)),


  #The plot created in server.R is displayed
    mainPanel(
      plotOutput("plot")
    )
  )
))
```

JavaScript

JavaScript can be included in a Shiny application in different ways. As script is available in the tags list, this can be included in a `script` tag. This is how the UI.R file would look like in this case:

```
library(shiny)

# Starting line
shinyUI(fluidPage(

  #JavaScript piece of code

  tags$head(tags$script(HTML("function changeColor(x,y){
    x.style.backgroundColor = y;}"))),

  # Application title
  titlePanel("Example 1"),

  sidebarLayout(

    # Sidebar with a numeric input
    sidebarPanel(
      numericInput("number",
        "Insert a number:",
        value = 30,
        min = 1,
        max = 50)
      ),


    #The plot created in server.R is displayed
    mainPanel(
      plotOutput("plot")
    )
  )
))
```

In this example, it was necessary to enclose the JavaScript in HTML(), a function that indicates that the string enclosed in it must be treated as an HTML code. Otherwise, this would be treated as normal text and consequently would not be executed.

The JavaScript code inserted produces, at this stage, no change. If the application was executed with the UI.R file detailed previously, there would be no difference because the JavaScript code inserted is just a function declaration, but the function is not called anywhere. This function receives two arguments, an HTML element and a color name, and changes the color of the HTML element to the color passed.

As it happens with tags functions, some additional arguments can be passed to other widgets as well, which will be treated as attributes of the corresponding HTML tag. It is worth mentioning that some of these have certain restrictions with respect to the arguments they accept. In the following UI.R code, a mouseover and mouseout argument will be added to sidebarPanel(), whose value will be a call to the JavaScript function previously explained:

```
library(shiny)

# Starting line
shinyUI(fluidPage(

#JavaScript piece of code

  tags$head(tags$script(HTML("function changeColor(x,y){
    x.style.backgroundColor = y;}"))),

  # Application title
  titlePanel("Example 1"),

  sidebarLayout(

  # Sidebar with a numeric input

  sidebarPanel(
    onmouseover = 'changeColor(this,"blue")',
    onmouseout ='changeColor(this,"gray")',
    style = 'background-color: gray',
    numericInput("number",
      "Insert a number:",
      value = 30,
      min = 1,
      max = 50)
  ),

    #The plot created in server.R is displayed
    mainPanel(
```

```
        plotOutput ("plot")
    )
   )
 ))
```

When a function is called inside an argument, it is not necessary to enclose the JavaScript function in HTML(). However, it is still necessary to pass this as a string.

Scripts can be included from source too. In order to do this, the file that is called has to be stored inside the www folder. Back to the previous example, if the function was saved in a file named change_color.js, the corresponding call in UI.R would be as follows:

```
tags$head(tags$script(src="change_color.js"))
```

CSS

Apart from including custom JavaScript, tags are very useful to include CSS as well. **CSS** stands for **Cascading Style Sheet** and it enables the definition of specifications regarding the style of the different elements in the HTML document, such as font type, font size, background color, and text align. CSS is ideal, for example, for specifying that all divs in a page should be in red.

In general terms, the inclusion of CSS in UI.R is similar to JavaScript; either by specifying the CSS code directly, or by reference to an external file either with an src argument in tags$style() or through the includeCSS() function. For the first case, the code would be as follows:

```
tags$head(tags$style(HTML(
  "body{
    background-color: LightGray;}

  h2{
    font-family: Arial;
    color: red;}"

)))
```

If we store the CSS code (the one enclosed in the HTML() function in the following example) in a file and call it with includeCSS(), this will done as follows:

```
includeCSS("example_1.css")
```

Other tags

Although the possibility of including CSS and JavaScript in a Shiny application without needing to generate HTML from scratch enables a developer to customize almost everything in the application's UI directly from the UI.R, functions in the tags object can be very useful to generate other HTML tags as well (for instance, divs, titles, and so on). For example, in this piece of code, a small blue text is added after the numeric input:

```
sidebarPanel(
  numericInput("number",
  "Insert a number:",
  value = 30,
  min = 1,
  max = 50),
  tags$p(style="color:blue","This is some additional blue text")
),
```

Again, style can be passed without any problems as an argument to any function that creates a container (for example, sidebarPanel(), mainPanel(), tags$div(), tags$p(), and so on). However, when it comes to customizing inputs, for example, it is sometimes necessary to use bootstrapPage() instead of fluidPage() or fixedPage().

In this case, passing style directly as an argument is not possible and a piece of the corresponding CSS code has to be added, in any of the preceding methods. This relies on the fact that both fluidPage() and fixedPage() load their own CSS stylesheet that prevail over the one given by the user. In this sense, it has to be considered that all the other style elements that come along with a fluid or fixed page will not be applied (for instance, margins). The following is an example of how the code will be in UI.R:

```
library(shiny)

# Starting line
shinyUI(bootstrapPage(

  #CSS to change "number's" background color
  tags$head(tags$style(HTML("#number {background-color: yellow;}"))),

  # Application title

  titlePanel("Example 1"),

  sidebarLayout(
```

```
  # Sidebar with a numeric input

  sidebarPanel(
    numericInput("number",
    "Insert a number:",
    value = 30,
    min = 1,
    max = 50)
  ),


  #The plot created in server.R is displayed
  mainPanel(
    plotOutput("plot")
  )
 )
))
```

In the preceding example, the background of the input widget is yellow because the CSS code specifies that the style has to be applied to the element with ID number. This specification is done by including # and the ID name.

To conclude, it is worth talking about withTags(). This is a function that refers to every function called inside it as a part of the tags object. Back to the second JavaScript example:

tags$head(tags$script(src="change_color.js"))

This is equivalent to:

```
withTags(
  head(
    script(src="change_color.js")))
```

 The sole purpose of this function is to avoid writing tags$ every time a function inside the tags object is called.

The most important concept that underlies this section is that although sometimes the methods are not equivalent, the Shiny applications provide the possibility of performing a selective customization of almost every single item in the application's frontend without the need to code an entire HTML document, which can be a very difficult task to complete for those who are not proficient with frontend web development.

Probably the most important advantage of using R code, at least to structure the frontend, relies on the fact that the communication between the backend and the frontend is completely assured and handled directly by R without any need for special developments.

Relating HTML/JavaScript and server.R

As it was mentioned earlier, one of the biggest advantages of customizing the application UI by just adding tags to UI.R becomes even more visible when the user interface elements (HTML, JavaScript, and so on) depend on reactive values too. This case of reactivity is definitely different from the ones seen so far as the output should be included as HTML code, especially when it comes to JavaScript. For this kind of situation, session$sendCustomMessage() along with a built-in JavaScript function, Shiny.addCustomMessageHandler(), have to be used.

Basically, the first function sends a message to the user interface that will be based on reactive inputs. The second function listens to this and acts accordingly. Considering the JavaScript example again, the following code produces an application where if the input variable (input$number) is less than or equal to 25, the mouseover/mouseout colors will be blue or gray respectively, while if the input value is greater than 25, the color pair will be red/green.

As you might have already noticed, these kinds of customizations need to be similar to the update functions, the invocation of a session object. This object contains by default sendCustomMessage(). This function has two arguments: type and the values to be passed to UI.R. This last argument is packed in a JSON format and delivered to the handler, which can perform the JavaScript operations based on this. The following is the code for this in server.R:

```
library(shiny)

#initialization of server.R
shinyServer(function(input, output,session) {

  observe({
    input$number
    colorover <- ifelse(input$number <= 25,"blue","red")
    colorout <- ifelse(input$number <= 25,"gray","green")
    session$sendCustomMessage(type='updatecolors',
list(over=colorover,out =colorout))
  })

  #Plot generation
  output$plot <- renderPlot({
```

```
      plot(1/1:input$number)
  })
```

```
})
```

In the following UI.R code, Shiny.addCustomMessageHandler() is passed as an inline script but it can be included in any of the ways described in this chapter. Shiny.addCustomMessageHandler() receives two parameters:

- Firstly, a string that defines the type (that is, the type specified in the corresponding session$sendCustomMessage() on the server side)
- Secondly, a function where the output produced on the server side can be included within a JavaScript code.

As it was already explained, the objects generated by session$sendCustomMessage() are passed to UI as a JSON object. For this reason, the call is done as function_argument.value. The name of this argument in the function passed to Shiny.addCustomMessageHandler() can be anything. This is the name that the object that is returned on the server side will acquire in the UI.

The following is the UI.R script:

```
library(shiny)

# Starting line
shinyUI(bootstrapPage(

  tags$head(tags$script(src="change_color.js")),

  tags$head(tags$script(HTML(
    ' var colorover;
    var colorout ;
    Shiny.addCustomMessageHandler("updatecolors",
    function(color) { colorover= String(color.over);
    colorout= String(color.out)});'
  ))),

  # Application title
  titlePanel("Example 1"),
```

```
# Sidebar with a numeric input
# Sidebar
sidebarLayout(
  sidebarPanel(
    onmouseover = 'changeColor(this,colorover)',
    onmouseout = 'changeColor(this,colorout)',
    style = "background-color: green;",
    numericInput("number",
    "Insert a number:",
    value = 30,
    min = 1,
    max = 50)),


    #The plot created in server.R is displayed
    mainPanel(
      plotOutput("plot")
    )
  )
))
```

In this example, two variables were created to store the color value that will be passed afterwards to changeColor(), the same function that was created for the previous example. The values of these variables are updated by Shiny. addCustomMessageHandler() based on the output received from the server.

The calls to the arguments of changeColor(), onmouseover and onmouseout, change only in their second argument where, instead of having a fixed string, colorover and colorout is passed to them respectively. The JavaScript variables in this case have to be declared outside Shiny.addCustomMessageHandler() due to scope as, similar to R, the variables declared inside a function cannot be called from outside.

With these two scripts plus change_color.js from the previous example, it should be enough to generate an application where, if input$number is greater than 25, the input panel should be either red or green (depending on whether the cursor is inside the box or not), or gray or blue if input$number is less than or equal to 25.

Summary

In this chapter, advanced alternatives combining HTML, JavaScript, and CSS with Shiny were covered. Although the learning curve of these types of problems is definitely hard, the effort is worth it, as this opens an infinite number of new gates.

The next chapter will cover the different alternatives of interaction with output objects and will focus on the inclusion of interaction within native R graphics and the integration between Shiny and D3, a very popular JavaScript library to produce graphical elements. For this reason, it is important that the contents of this chapter are solidly understood, at least from a conceptual point of view. The final aim is, in the end, the same that guides the principles of Shiny, that is, to get the best out of the two worlds: web applications for the display of results and a powerful data processing/analysis engine behind to produce insightful and novel information.

Interactive Graphics in Shiny

9

This chapter briefly covers two main possibilities of adding interactivity to the graphics in a Shiny application: by including interaction possibilities for native R graphics provided by the Shiny package, or by integrating JavaScript-generated visualizations, which can be interactive. Although some of the libraries seen in this book such as googleVis are interactive, their interaction is already specified. For example, on hovering it is not possible on googleVis to do something else different from displaying a tooltip. The two solutions presented here are much more flexible in this sense because the developer can receive the information from the interaction and produce any kind of reaction to it.

Interaction possibilities within R graphics

From Shiny 0.12, it has been possible to develop applications with graphics or images that are responsive to interactions. Its implementation is very simple, as the interaction events are tracked as any other input objects and behave in the exact same way. Until the 0.12 version, there have been four basic interaction events. In order to listen to them, the corresponding argument must be specified to the plotting function where the value of this argument is the corresponding listener. The following are the events:

- **Hover**: This tracks the position of the mouse. The argument to be passed is hover and the function is hoverOpts().

- **Click**: This tracks the position of the click. The argument is click and the function is clickOpts().

- **Double click**: This tracks the position of the double-click. The argument is dblclick and the function is dblClickOpts().

- **Brush**: This tracks the brushed area. The argument is brush and the function is brushOpts().

A single string can be passed instead of the complete function to each of the arguments previously mentioned. In this case, a listener with that ID will be created. In any case, the listener will be accessible on the server side with the `input$(listener_ id)` form. This object will be of `list` type and will have a series of values according to its nature. A good example of what each of them returns can be found at `http://shiny.rstudio.com/ gallery/plot-interaction-basic.html`.

Take into account that this feature works optimally with the latest version of Shiny and `htmlwidgets`, a package that will be introduced in the next section. Updating a package in R is done in the exact same way as installing them.

The following example illustrates the use of this functionality of brush on the `iris` dataset. Basically, a plot is displayed and the brushed points appear in the table below. For this particular case, the high level `brushedPoints()` function is used. This function takes a brush listener and a data frame object and automatically generates a subset of the selected points in a data frame:

This is for `global.R`:

```
data(iris)
```

The following snippet is for `UI.R`:

```
library(shiny)

# Starting line
shinyUI(fluidPage(

  # Application title
  titlePanel("Example 1"),

  sidebarLayout(

  # Sidebar with a numeric input
    sidebarPanel(
      selectInput("var1", "Select variable 1", names(iris)),
      selectInput("var2", "Select variable 2", names(iris))
    ),


    #The plot created in server.R is displayed
      mainPanel(
        plotOutput("plot",brush = brushOpts(
```

```
        id = "plot_brush")),
      tableOutput("selectedpoints")
    )
  )
))
```

The only change with respect to UI files seen so far is that the `brush` argument is added to `plotOutput()`. In this case, the full `brushOpts()` function was used. The following is for `server.R`:

```
library(shiny)

#initialization of server.R
shinyServer(function(input, output) {

  #Plot generation
  output$plot <- renderPlot({
    selected.vars <- c(input$var1, input$var2)

    plot(iris[,c(selected.vars)])
  })

  output$selectedpoints <- renderTable({

    return(brushedPoints(iris,input$plot_brush, xvar = input$var1,
yvar = input$var2))

  })

})
```

Inside `renderTable()`, the mentioned high-level function was used specifying the dataset, event listener, and corresponding horizontal and vertical variable names. This section can also be rewritten as:

```
iris.sset <- iris[,iris[[input$var1]] >= input$plot_brush$xmin &
  iris[[input$var1]] <= input$plot_brush$xmax &
  iris[[input$var2]] >= input$plot_brush$ymin &
  iris[[input$var2]] <= input$plot_brush$ymax]
return(iris.sset)
```

This is how the application should look:

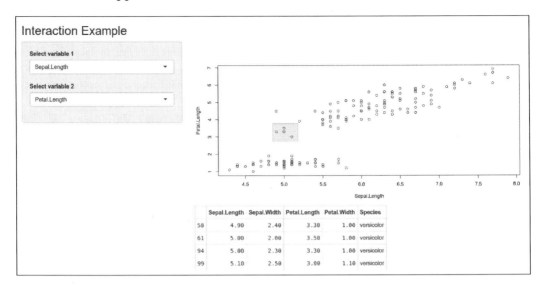

In the next section, we will cover how to generate custom functions that render JavaScript-based elements. From all the possibilities, only D3 will be covered.

D3.js integration

This is naturally perfectly possible as D3 visualizations are HTML/JavaScript-based, and as it was already explained in this book, Shiny applications can support this type of content without any problems.

This section will have three main subsections:

- What is D3.js?
- networkD3
- An introduction to `htmlwidgets`

What is D3?

D3.js is a JavaScript library designed by Mike Bostock. As with any other library in any other language (for example, R), D3 contains a set of functions written in JavaScript that are especially used for visualizations.

The name of this library is an acronym for **Data-Driven Documents** (three times the letter D) and its name is self-explanatory of the purpose of the library's functions, that is, to produce HTML documents based on data given. Of course, this data can change, and the HTML rendered has to change accordingly.

This kind of process should sound familiar to every reader at this point; graphical objects that change according to the interaction with the end user, just like Shiny's input-output logic. So, if D3's logic closely resembles that of Shiny and Shiny's user interface is an HTML document (as it was explained many times, UI.R produces an HTML document in the end), including D3 objects into a Shiny application is something that many developers will want to do.

 The D3 visualizations are widely used due to the interaction possibilities that it provides, for example, by clicking on a certain element of the graph and expecting something to happen, such as selecting the cases that correspond to that item, zooming in, and tooltipping.

D3 takes JSON objects as data input. **JSON** is an acronym that stands for **JavaScript Object Notation** and is basically a nonstructured data storage format. JSON is widely used in various types of applications, especially in JavaScript-based ones, such as Shiny and D3. In the introduction to htmlwidgets in this section, this topic will be covered. htmlwidgets is a package that enables us to generate packages with JavaScript codes especially designed to be used in Shiny applications.

However, before deep diving into this package, let's take a look at a finished package done with htmlwidgets to create network graphs in D3.

networkD3

As its name indicates, networkD3 is a library to generate network graphs in D3. Once these kinds of packages are generated, there is no need to write JavaScript or D3 code, as this is solved directly by the package. Network graphs visually describe the relationship between nodes.

This particular library includes Reingold-Tilford tree network diagrams and simple network visualizations. All of them include interactivity possibilities typical from D3 visualizations. In the case of the Reingold-Tilford tree, the name of the node is zoomed with mouseover. In the case of the classical network, it can be moved and turned around by clicking at one of its points and dragging it around the window.

In the preceding example, an artificial dataset consisting of four nodes, a, b, c, and d, is generated and a network graph is consequently created. For this, `simpleNetwork()` is used. This function expects a 3-variable dataset where the two first are the nodes being linked and the third one is the edge value:

```
library(networkD3)

a <- c("a","b","a","c","b")
b <- c("b","d","c","d","c")
c <- c(1,4,5,2,4)

sample <- data.frame(a,b,c)
simpleNetwork(sample)
```

This script will generate an interactive network graph in the viewer pane. As it can be seen in the package's documentation, many look-and-feel features such as nodes' colors and font sizes can be customized.

In the case of Reingold-Tilford trees, the input data requires a fixed format. This relies on the fact that the original D3 function used for this visualization already expects a JSON with a fixed format; a parent-child structure where the node's children are grouped in an object named `children`. Of course, the children nodes can have their own children nodes inside them. This kind of structure is easily adaptable to R, as the list format is perfectly capable of supporting this nested structure. This is the reason why the function that generates this visualization (`treeNetwork()`) expects a list with this structure, which is converted internally to a JSON document and passed to the D3 function.

In the following example, a visualization of some of the world's countries is done. Similar to the previous example, almost all the look-and-feel features are customizable:

```
library(networkD3)

world <- list(name="World", children=list(

  list(name="America", children = list(
    list(name="Argentina"),
    list(name="Brazil"),
    list(name="Uruguay")
  )),
  list(name="Africa", children = list(
    list(name="Benin"),
```

```
      list(name="Argelia"),
      list(name="South Africa")
    )),
    list(name="Europe", children = list(
      list(name="Germany"),
      list(name="Italy"),
      list(name="Spain")
    )),
    list(name="Asia", children = list(
      list(name="Japan"),
      list(name="China"),
      list(name="India")
    ))
  ))
```

```
  treeNetwork(world, fontSize=15)
```

The reader might have noticed at this point that the visualizations returned by this package are not images; they are HTML documents that produce a visualization. Due to this, it is not possible to include them in a Shiny application in the same way as ordinary plots are included. All the graphical features generated with `htmlwidgets` have their own render and output functions.

In the following example, the Reingold-Trifford graph created previously is included in an application where the continents can be selected.

As the graph's input will always be fractions of the same object, this is declared in `global.R`:

```
  library(networkD3)

  world <- list(name="World", children=list(

  list(name="America", children = list(
    list(name="Argentina"),
    list(name="Brazil"),
    list(name="Uruguay")
  )),
  list(name="Africa", children = list(
    list(name="Benin"),
    list(name="Argelia"),
    list(name="South Africa")
  )),
  list(name="Europe", children = list(
    list(name="Germany"),
```

```
      list(name="Italy"),
      list(name="Spain")
    )),
    list(name="Asia", children = list(
      list(name="Japan"),
      list(name="China"),
      list(name="India")
    ))
  ))
))
```

As it was already explained, D3Network has its own set of output functions (one for each visualization). In this case, treeNetworkOutput is used. Have a look at the following code snippet for UI.R:

```
library(shiny)

# Starting line
shinyUI(fluidPage(

  # Application title
  titlePanel("Graph Example"),

  sidebarLayout(

  # Sidebar with a numeric input

    sidebarPanel(
      checkboxGroupInput("continents", "Choose the continents",
                         choices = c("Africa","America","Asia","Euro
pe"),
                         selected = c("Africa","America","Asia","Euro
pe"))
    ),


  #The plot created in server.R is displayed
    mainPanel(
      treeNetworkOutput("graph")
    )
  )
))
```

In `server.R`, some processing was necessary in order to generate the plot. In fact, the object selection recreates the `world` primary object by keeping its name and the children whose `name` subitem matches with the names selected that is stored in `input$continents`:

```
library(shiny)

#initialization of server.R
shinyServer(function(input, output) {

  selections <- reactive({
    selected.continents <- sapply(world$children, "[[", "name") %in%
input$continents
    list(name=world$name, children = world$children[selected.
continents])
    })


  #Plot generation
  output$graph <- renderTreeNetwork({
    treeNetwork(selections(),fontSize = 20)})

})
```

Finally in the plot production, it is important to notice that, although it might seem redundant, it is necessary to include both `renderTreeNetwork()` and `treeNetwork()` because `renderTreeNetwork()` is the render function for this type of visualization. Similar to any other render function, `renderTreeNetwork()` does not produce any output; it just generates the conditions for its display. It is the `treeNetwork()` function that actually generates the code for the plot.

An introduction to htmlwidgets

`htmlwidgets` is a package intended to help developers to include their custom JavaScript code to generate visualizations in R by creating special libraries. Based on file templates, it facilitates the linking between both languages. Although this package is not dependent on `devtools`, the latter library is necessary to build the package, that is, to generate the package from a series of source codes. The installation is performed in the exact same way:

```
install.packages("devtools")
install.packages("htmlwidgets")
```

For this section, D3.js will be used, which is a JavaScript library to do visualizations. Learning D3.js is a task that is completely beyond the scope of this book. For this reason, the example that will be presented here will be kept extremely simple, as it will just illustrate some concepts of how to do this.

It is recommended for readers who would like to include D3 or any other JavaScript visualization library in their Shiny application, to look for specific material on these as rather than focus on explaining D3, this section will focus on how to integrate JavaScript to a Shiny app. For this reason, the D3 code used in this example will not be explained.

Let's follow the instructions given in the package webpage (`www.htmlwidgets.org`) to generate the files with slight changes:

1. Load the libraries, `htmlwdgets` and `devtools`:

   ```
   library(htmlwidgets)
   library(devtools)
   ```

2. Create the `package` project. In this case, it will be named `D3BarChart`:

   ```
   create("D3BarChart")
   ```

   This command generates a project folder with the minimum necessary files to build any package in R, a `DESCRIPTION` file (used to establish certain specifications about the package that will not be used in this example), a `NAMESPACE` file and an R folder where the files that contain the package's source codes are included. After creating the project, we can access the folder and see the mentioned files:

   ```
   setwd("D3BarChart")
   list.files()
   [1] "D3BarChart.Rproj" "DESCRIPTION"    "NAMESPACE"    "R"
   ```

In this case, no edition will be done on these files. However, this is not true in every case. For more details on writing custom libraries in R, you can read CRAN's documentation from `http://cran.r-project.org/doc/manuals/r-release/R-exts.html` or Hadley's Wickham book exclusively dedicated to this issue available at `http://r-pkgs.had.co.nz/`.

3. Once the project is created and we are in the project's folder (see the preceding `setwd()` statement), we will run `scaffoldWidget()`, a function from the `htmlwidget` package that generates the necessary files to develop our JavaScript integrated package:

```
scaffoldWidget("D3BarChart")
```

In RStudio, the generated files will be opened by default, as shown here:

```
D3BarChart.yaml ×    D3BarChart.js ×    D3BarChart.R ×

     Source on Save                                        Run       Source

 1   #' <Add Title>
 2   #'
 3   #' <Add Description>
 4   #'
 5   #' @import htmlwidgets
 6   #'
 7   #' @export
 8   D3BarChart <- function(message, width = NULL, height = NULL) {
 9
10     # forward options using x
11     x = list(
12       message = message
13     )
14
15     # create widget
16     htmlwidgets::createWidget(
17       name = 'D3BarChart',
18       x,
19       width = width,
20       height = height,
1:1   (Top Level)                                              R Script
```

After these steps, the entire necessary structure is, in principle, ready to generate our package. Let's take a look at each of the generated files first and understand what is in them.

D3BarChart.R

As in any other package, source files are stored in a subdirectory called R in the project's folder. The name of the file is generated by default with respect to the name passed when the package project was created. Inside this file, we will, firstly, see the header, which is a specification done on the roxygen syntax about the package imports. These are the libraries that contain all the necessary functions for the package being created.

It is important to consider that using the `library()` function inside the package source files is not possible. The `export` tag specifies the functions that will confirm the package. For more information about roxygen, visit `http://roxygen.org/roxygen.pdf`.

The first of the functions declared is the actual builder, that is, the one that will interact with the JavaScript code and generate the corresponding HTML/JavaScript document. Its first argument (message) is a part of the default example. Inside this, an object named x is created with the actual arguments that will be passed afterwards to the JavaScript function. By default, it contains the message object declared previously. This will be changed when we create our own function to meet the needs of it.

Next, a call to createWidget() is done. This function is basically responsible for creating the whole HTML/JavaScript document based on the .js file, which will be explained in the following section. One of the arguments in this function call is a list containing the necessary parameters to be passed to the JavaScript code, which are stored, by default, in this object named x.

Finally, two more functions are declared to include the generated visualizations in a Shiny application: the render and the output function. There is no need to edit anything here.

D3BarChart.js

This file is located in the inst/htmlwidgets directory tree inside the project's folder. It has three functions declared by default: initialize(), renderValue(), and resize(). In the first one, objects that are needed but not dependent on our data can be initialized, for example, a container. This function takes as arguments width and height from the createWidget() call.

In renderValue(), all the data dependent objects in the visualization are included. As it can be seen, renderValue() takes the x list as one of its arguments. All the subitems of the x list object can be accessed in a JavaScript way, that is, as x (the name of the element). For this reason, it is always advisable when working on these types of visualizations, to avoid passing elements whose names may contain dots. Lastly, resize() is intended to contain the pieces of code to rearrange items if the container's size changes.

D3BarChart.yaml

The YAML files are placed under the same directory as the .js file and are responsible for the definition of HTML dependencies for the corresponding package. The dependencies specified here are not R related and can refer, for example, to JavaScript libraries, CSS stylesheets, and so on.

Now that we have a certain understanding of each of the necessary source files to build a custom JavaScript-based widget, let's generate a widget. This example will be simply a bar chart for the specified variable with blue fills and red contours and a tooltip on mouse positioning over the bars. This example will be developed using the D3.js library. In this case, the arguments to be passed will be a data frame, the plotting numeric variable's name in a string format, and the name of the variable appearing in the tooltip passed as a string as well.

Let's focus on the R file first. This is the code for it in `D3BarChart.R`:

```
#' <Add Title>
#'
#' <Add Description>
#'
#' @import htmlwidgets
#'
#' @export
D3BarChart <- function(data,var,tooltip, width = NULL, height = NULL)
{

  # forward options using x
  x = list(
    inpdata = data,
    plotvar = var,
    tooltip = tooltip
  )

  # create widget
  htmlwidgets::createWidget(
    name = 'D3BarChart',
    x,
    width = width,
    height = height,
    package = 'D3BarChart'
  )
}

#' Widget output function for use in Shiny
#'
#' @export
D3BarChartOutput <- function(outputId, width = '100%', height =
'400px'){
  shinyWidgetOutput(outputId, 'D3BarChart', width, height, package =
'D3BarChart')
```

```
}

#' Widget render function for use in Shiny
#'
#' @export
renderD3BarChart <- function(expr, env = parent.frame(), quoted =
FALSE) {
    if (!quoted) { expr <- substitute(expr) } # force quoted
    shinyRenderWidget(expr, D3BarChartOutput, env, quoted = TRUE)
}
```

The arguments of the main function call have been changed according to the actual needs of the function and naturally included in the x object. The rest remained default.

In D3BarChart.yaml, two dependencies will need to be specified; firstly, the reference to the D3 JavaScript library that we will be using, and then a reference to a CSS file that defines the styles of the tooltip's divs.

All the libraries used must be locally accessible and within the project's folder. For this reason, we have to download the library from https://github.com/mbostock/d3/zipball/master. From all the downloaded files, only d3.min.js is needed. For this example, the file is copied to /inst/htmlwidgets/libraries. The CSS file will be named divstyle.css and stored under the /inst/htmlwidgets/styles directory. The file looks as follows:

```
.tooltips {position: fixed;
         text-align: center;
         width: 80px;
         height: 50px;
         padding: 2px;
         font: 12px sans-serif;
         color: white;
         background: red;
         border: 0px;
         border-radius: 8px;
         left: 0;
         top:0;
         display:none; }
```

The YAML file must consequently specify the dependencies of both the JavaScript library and the CSS file. So this is how it looks like in D3BarChart.yaml:

```yaml
dependencies:
  - name: d3
    version: 3.5.6
    src: "htmlwidgets/libraries"
    script: d3.min.js
  - name: divstyle
    version: 0.0.1
    src: "htmlwidgets/styles"
stylesheet: divstyle.css
```

 Notice that in this case, as the YAML file is also in the inst directory, only the references in src from that point are needed to be specified.

Finally, it is time to code the actual JavaScript visualization. In this case, neither initialization nor resizing are required, as the size of the widget is directly dependent on the size of its container and is declared inside renderValue().

The following is the code of the entire JavaScript section in D3BarChart.js:

```javascript
HTMLWidgets.widget({

    name: 'D3BarChart',

    type: 'output',

    initialize: function(el, width, height) {

        return {};

    },

    renderValue: function(el, x, instance) {

// Variable definitions

    var jsdata = HTMLWidgets.dataframeToD3(x.inpdata);
    var hei = el.offsetHeight/jsdata.length;
    var maxwid = Math.max.apply(Math,jsdata.map(function(o){return
eval('o.' + x                    .plotvar)}));
    var y = d3.scale.linear()
                .domain([0, maxwid])
```

```
                .range([0, el.offsetWidth]);
     var tooltipsdiv = d3.select(el)
                 .append("div")
                 .attr("class", "tooltips");


//Remove old widget. Important for Shiny Applications.

d3.select(el).select("svg").remove();

//Rectangles drawings

        d3.select(el)
        .append("svg")
        .attr("width", el.offsetWidth)
        .attr("height", el.offsetHeight)
        .selectAll("rect")
        .data(jsdata)
        .enter()
        .append("rect")
        .attr("width", function(d) { return y(eval('d.' + x.plotvar));
})
        .attr("height", hei)
        .attr("transform", function(d,i) { return "translate(0," + i *
hei + ")"; })
        .attr("style", "fill:blue; stroke:white")
        .on("mouseover", function(d) {
          tooltipsdiv
     .attr("style", "display: block; left: " + d3.event.pageX + "px;
top: " + d3            .event.pageY + "px;")
            .text(x.tooltip + " : " + eval("d." + x.tooltip));
                                   })
        .on("mouseout", function(d) {
            tooltipsdiv
        .attr("style", "display: none;")
        ;});


  },

  resize: function(el, width, height, instance) {


  }

});
```

It is out of the scope of this book to go deeper into the JavaScript code. However, from this particular example, it is just worth pointing out that it is necessary to include a line to remove the previous svg containers, that is, where the elements are drawn because if they are included in a Shiny application, the function will attach the plot to the widget area instead of replacing it whenever the visualization is re-rendered.

Once all the files are ready, it is time to build the package. Since our active directory is one of the packages, we have to run install() from package devtools.

This is the final console output that you should be getting:

```
* installing *source* package 'D3BarChart' ...
** R
** inst
** preparing package for lazy loading
** help
No man pages found in package  'D3BarChart'
*** installing help indices
** building package indices
** testing if installed package can be loaded
*** arch - i386
*** arch - x64
* DONE (D3BarChart)
```

The library should now be available for use with the rest of the libraries and can be called in the exact same way. As it was said, the widget can be now called individually, as follows:

```
> sample.data.frame <- data.frame(numvar = 1:10, catvar =
LETTERS[1:10])
> D3BarChart(sample.data.frame,"numvar","catvar")
```

This is the output:

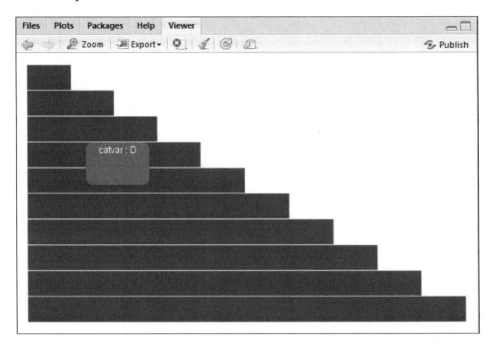

Alternatively, this can be done inside a Shiny application with the special render and output functions generated automatically by `htmlwidgets`. The following is a small example with the `iris` dataset where the mean by species of the selected variable is displayed:

The following is the code for `global.R`:

```
library(D3BarChart)
library(htmlwidgets)
data(iris)

names(iris) <- gsub("\\.","",names(iris))

aggreg.iris <- aggregate(.~Species,data = iris,  FUN = mean)
```

In `global.R`, the dots are taken out from the names because of their potential conflicts with JavaScript's syntax where the dot has a special meaning. After this, the aggregation is precalculated prior to the application's load.

The code for `UI.R` is as follows:

```
library(shiny)

    # Starting line
  shinyUI(fluidPage(

    # Application title
    titlePanel("Example with D3BarChart"),

    sidebarLayout(

    sidebarPanel(

        #Species selection
      selectInput("var1","Select variable:",
                    choices = setdiff(names(aggreg.iris),"Species"),
selected = NULL)),

    mainPanel(
      #The plot is displayed via the special function

    D3BarChartOutput("plot1")
    )
  )
))
```

The UI structure in this case is very simple; just one input value and one output whose output function is `D3BarChartOutput()`.

Finally, `server.R` looks like this:

```
library(shiny)

#initialization of server.R
shinyServer(function(input, output) {


  #Plots generation
  output$plot1 <- renderD3BarChart(

    D3BarChart(aggreg.iris, input$var1, "Species")
  )

})
```

On the server side, both `D3BarChart()` and `renderD3BarChart()` are used. As it happened with D3Network and with any other plotting function used in Shiny, it is necessary to have both the functions do the output and render this in the application.

As it can be seen, the R code for the inclusion of user-defined JavaScript visualizations is very simple. Mastering JavaScript is definitely the challenge when developing these kinds of custom visualizations.

Summary

Interaction with graphics, either through Shiny's built-in listeners or through JavaScript integration, is the last topic related to specifically developing applications in Shiny. It is supposed that, after these nine chapters, the reader has acquired the main concepts required to code their own applications. Of course, the world of R and web programming (HTML, JavaScript, and so on) is infinite and impossible to cover thoroughly in a book. For this reason, this book intends to be a guide for the reader to understand the scope and possibilities of creating web applications in R, and from here, make their own path through a universe full of different possibilities.

The next chapter will cover the different of sharing your application, which is the reason why we create them; to expose information to people who, for any reason, cannot obtain it themselves.

10
Sharing Applications

After covering the most important issues regarding the programming of a Shiny application, it is now necessary to introduce the different possibilities of fulfilling the main purpose of developing a Shiny application, that is, exhibiting it.

In this chapter, we will look at the different ways of sharing an application, that is, from simply passing the code files to setting up a web address to make it accessible to anyone capable of connecting to it.

In this sense, it is important to keep in mind that in the majority of cases, it will be intended to make these applications accessible to everyone, regardless of their programming skills or the software they have installed on their computers. Although this might sound trivial or obvious, doing this optimally implies that certain specific knowledge is required to configure the applications correctly.

Once the application is ready, there are mainly four ways of sharing it as follows:

- **Passing the whole code**: This is as easy as zipping the application and sending it over the Internet. This is naturally one of the worst alternatives and is only sensible, for instance, to share the application with a colleague or co-worker. In many cases, it is not even the best alternative, as using version control is definitely better. In this case, it will be necessary that the person who receives these files has all the corresponding software (R and RStudio, at least) installed and all the required packages along with a certain expertise in R in order to reproduce the application and run it locally.

- **runGist/runGitHub/runUrl**: This Shiny package provides certain alternatives to run applications whose files are hosted on the Internet locally, by passing either `gist`, a GitHub repository directory, or a URL that points to a compressed file (`.tar.gz`, `.tar`, and `.zip` extensions are accepted). Although this is definitely better in terms of sharing simplicity than the previous alternative, they are essentially the same.

- **shinyapps.io**: Under http://www.shinyapps.io/, RStudio provides a hosting service especially prepared for Shiny applications. Its main advantage relies on the simplicity to manage them; uploading applications from your local machine will take no longer than 5 minutes. Apart from this, it provides a very intuitive and friendly GUI to administrate users, permissions, and so on. Probably, its main drawback is that the free version is limited (in terms of hours of service, storage, and so on) and that the developer has naturally no access to the configuration options of the server that is hosting the application. From the end user side, it is only needed that they have a compatible web browser.

- **Own server**: Hosting applications on your own server is also a possibility. In this case, the end user requirements are the same as in the case of shinyapps.io. In comparison, hosting applications on your own server is an advantage in the sense that the open version has no time restrictions, and for advanced users, this can provide some extra customizing possibilities. However, naturally, its configuration is entirely manual. The paid version offers some considerable extra features as well.

In the following, the details of each of the alternatives presented will be given, except for the first one, which is actually something widely known by every Internet user.

runGist/runGitHub/runUrl

These three functions provided by Shiny basically do the same. In fact, runGist() and runGitHub() are mere wrappers of runUrl(). They basically build the URL based on GitHub's standard taxonomy and call runUrl(). All these functions download all the files to a temporary folder on the local computer and execute them on the end user's side. Of course, if the application requires any file that is not included in the repository, it must be on the user's side. If an application calls a library and it is not on the end user's side, R will throw an error.

Both runGist() and runGitHub() point to a repository in GitHub. The main difference between them is that the first one is not necessarily associated to a user while the second one does. Apart from this, the gist repositories are identified with ID while the GitHub repositories have a name associated to them. For this reason, runGitHub() expects both username and repository name. The following is an example of both functions running the same application; one is hosted in a gist repository and the other, under my personal GitHub repository:

```
runGist("1867aa4a401d9d1a9239")

runGitHub("Dashboard","nivangio")
```

shinyapps.io

Unlike older versions of RStudio's application hosting services (such as Spark or Glimmer), shinyapps.io does not provide a development environment in the cloud. For this reason, the user has to develop their applications entirely somewhere else (either locally or on another server) and then upload the applications to their shinyapps.io account. The following shows an outline of the necessary steps to do this:

1. Check whether you have the corresponding package builder in your operating system. This is basically a compiler that will be used by R in order to build the packages.

2. Install `devtools`. This is a package that is included in CRAN, the official R repository, to develop and distribute packages that are not available in CRAN. Among their functions, for example, `install_github` can be found, which installs a package from a GitHub repository. The installation command is the same for all the packages:

    ```
    install.packages("devtools")
    ```

3. The previous step was necessary mainly because hosting applications on shinyapps.io depends on a package that is not available in CRAN. So, after installing `devtools`, `install_github` has to be used:

    ```
    devtools::install_github('rstudio/shinyapps')
    ```

 This method of using functions has not been covered in this book. It is mainly an alternative to call a function from a specific package without needing to load it. This could be useful to run isolated commands but is not recommended when scripting.

4. Next, load the package.

5. Go to shinyapps.io and register for an account.

6. Once logged in, under the user's logo, there is a menu named **Tokens**. Here, you will get the token, secret key, and command to run on the machine from where you are going to deploy the applications. This is basically an OAuth method. Copy the command, paste it, and run it on your local RStudio. There is even a button to copy the command directly.

7. Finally, in order to upload the directory, execute `deployApp()`, which will upload the application's files to your shinyapps.io instance and if needed, will install the necessary packages in your instance. `deployApp()` expects a path to a directory. If nothing is passed, it takes the working directory as the default.

8. After the upload is complete, your application will be accessible at `https://` `(your user name).shinyapps.io/(application's folder name)/`.

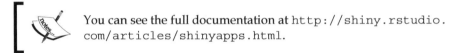

> You can see the full documentation at `http://shiny.rstudio.` `com/articles/shinyapps.html`.

Deploying applications on your own server

As it was previously mentioned, the Shiny applications can also be deployed on your own servers. However, there are still different versions of this; you can either use the open source version, which has certain limitations, or you can choose the paid one, which offers some extra capabilities such as user administration, password protecting, among others.

Keep in mind that the Shiny server is designed for Ubuntu, CentOS, and SUSE Linux Enterprise. Of course, the server instance where the applications will be hosted needs to have R, the RStudio server, and the Shiny package installed. It is important to keep in mind that all of these must be installed as superuser.

Installing R

The R installation on a server is identical to the R installation on a local computer. The following is an example in Ubuntu:

```
sudo apt-get install r-base
sudo apt-get install r-base-dev
```

For further information about these commands, see *Chapter 1, Introducing R, RStudio, and Shiny*.

Installing the RStudio server

Although the installation process is exactly the same as RStudio for local computers, the program to be downloaded is different and consequently, the link to download it is different as well. The following is an example in Ubuntu:

```
sudo apt-get install gdebi-core (avoid this step if you have already
gdebi-core installed)
wget https://download2.rstudio.org/rstudio-server-0.99.451-amd64.deb
sudo gdebi rstudio-server-0.99.451-amd64.deb
```

It is worth pointing out that installing RStudio will not only enable application hosting on your server, but will also give the possibility that every user in that VM can work in R with RStudio directly on the server from an ordinary browser, without needing to install R nor RStudio locally. The RStudio IDE serves normally on the `8787` port, so if the RStudio server is installed, it can be accessed by entering an address such as (IP of your server): `8787`

Installing the Shiny package

As the package will need to be accessible to every user, it will be necessary that it is installed as superuser as follows:

Initialize R as superuser directly from the console by typing the following:

`sudo R`

R will begin. After this, install Shiny as usual as follows:

`install.packages("shiny")`

In this way, Shiny will be installed through the `/usr/local/lib/R/site-library` path, which is accessible to every user on this server.

Regardless of whether it is a paid version or not, it is still quite simple, especially for those who have some experience with configuration in Linux environments. The following is an outline of the steps to follow.

Install the Shiny server by running the following commands:

`sudo apt-get install gdebi-core`

`wget https://download3.rstudio.org/ubuntu-12.04/x86_64/shiny-server-1.3.0.403-amd64.deb`

`sudo gdebi shiny-server-1.3.0.403-amd64.deb`

The first line could probably be avoided because `gdebi-core` was surely installed in the previous step.

The installation of the Shiny server will create a configuration file named `shiny-server.conf` under the `/etc/shiny-server/` path, where the configuration options of every application hosted in that server are specified. This is how it looks like by default:

```
# Instruct Shiny Server to run applications as the user "shiny"
run_as shiny;

# Define a server that listens on port 3838
```

```
server {
  listen 3838;

  # Define a location at the base URL
  location / {

    # Host the directory of Shiny Apps stored in this directory
    site_dir /srv/shiny-server;

    # Log all Shiny output to files in this directory
    log_dir /var/log/shiny-server;

    # When a user visits the base URL rather than a particular
application,
    # an index of the applications available in this directory will be
shown.
    directory_index on;
  }
}
```

 The full documentation is available under the following link:
`http://rstudio.github.io/shiny-server/latest/`.

The configuration is specified as `item value`, and as it can be observed, these specifications have a nested structure, which implies that every one of them is cascaded to the structures they contain, unless any of the child structures specify something different. In the following, you will find a small explanation of the most important configuration options:

- `run_as`
- `listen`
- `location`
- `site_dir/app_dir`
- `directory_index`

run_as

This is the username that the application will be running as. By default, the Shiny installation creates a generic user called `shiny`, which is the default for this field. In more concrete words, this means that whenever the application is used, it will be under the user stated in `run_as`. This is important because every user has their own library paths (accessible with `.libPaths()`).

So, if the user specified in `run_as` has no access to a library that is used in the application, it will probably throw an error related to this such as `There is no package called` .... To prevent this, the necessary packages should be installed as superuser in the same way that was explained before as this will install the package on a path that is included by default for every user:

```
sudo R
install.packages("package_to_install")
```

listen

This specifies the port where the applications will be listening. It is highly recommendable for non-expert users to keep the default, as the port numbers are usually associated with specific protocols. Changing this may lead to the malfunction of all the applications.

location

`location` defines a name where the application will be hosted. For example, if the location is specified as `/exampleApplication`, then it will be accessible with the default port listening under (the IP of the server): `3838/exampleApplication`.

site_dir/app_dir

These options are nested inside a location structure. Both specify a path where one or many applications reside. The main difference is that `site_dir` can contain multiple application directories while `app_dir` points to a specific application.

In the following, different configuration alternatives are presented for an imaginary situation where two application directories, `app1` and `app2`, are contained in the `/home/user1/applications` directory:

```
# Define a server that listens on port 3838
server {
  listen 3838;

  # Define a location at the base URL
  location /application1 {

    # Host the directory of Shiny Apps stored in this directory
    app_dir /home/user1/applications/app1;

  }
```

```
      location /application2 {

        # Host the directory of Shiny Apps stored in this directory
        app_dir /home/user1/applications/app2;

      }

   }
```

In this case, the applications will be accessible at (IP): 3838/application1 and (IP): 3838/application2, respectively.

A single location structure with site_dir can be used too as follows:

```
   # Define a server that listens on port 3838
   server {
     listen 3838;

     # Define a location at the base URL
     location /applications {

       # Host the directory of Shiny Apps stored in this directory
       site_dir /home/user1/applications/;

     }
   }
```

The URLs here would be (IP): 3838/applications/app1 and (IP): 3838/applications/app2. Note that in this case the URL ending points to the directory name of the particular application. This is because site_dir is replaced by the location specified, but the application's directory name remains.

directory_index

This specifies whether an index of applications available is shown when the user accesses the applications' base directories specified in site_dir. Looking back at the previous example, if the user accesses (IP): 3838/applications/, an index page showing the different applications will be displayed if directory_index is set to on.

Summary

This chapter has covered the most important aspects of how to share an application with R, and especially non-R, users. From the different alternatives presented here, hosting the application on a web server is particularly important, as it is probably the best way to share applications on the Internet. On the other hand, this is the one that requires more configuration, certain expertise, and, as usual, some trial and error.

The next and last chapter will be a step-by-step guide to code a sample application in R and Shiny, which will cover not only the code but the strategies used as well, the decisions taken, and so on. Thus from this book, you will not only have the guidelines for the necessary hard skills to code an application but also get an idea of, which are, conceptually, the best practices for these kinds of visualizations.

11
From White Paper to a Full Application

At this stage, it is supposed that the reader has already acquired enough technical knowledge to code a full application. This is naturally necessary to produce a successful output, but sometimes it is not enough. There are often thousands of different ways to get similar results in R or any other programming language. However, some of them are usually better than others in different ways: scalability, clearness, performance, timings, and so on.

In this chapter, an application is developed from scratch so that the reader comes face to face with a typical programmer's "real world" challenges where the pros and cons of different approaches are evaluated and decisions are taken with all their implications, that is, taking into account the possible drawbacks of the choices made. In this sense, the most important thing is to be conscious about all the strong points and especially, the weak points of your code.

This chapter will be divided into the following eight sections:

1. **Problem presentation**: The task is presented in a very realistic way as a boss or client would do.

2. **Conceptual design**: The central parts of the applications are thought of. In this part, it is not necessary to have a definite idea of all the application's functionalities, but it is recommended to have at least a clear idea of the inputs and outputs, for example, which variables will be filtered and which ones will be used to plot, general layout issues, and so on.

3. **Pre-application processing**: Based on the conceptual design, it is possible that some of the necessary processing (for example, aggregations) can be done before coding the application itself. Although this can be possibly avoided and included somewhere else (for example, in step 4 or 6), this step can lead to very significant improvements in terms of performance (some processes are run only once and not in real time, whenever someone calls the application or performs an action in it) and memory usage (the data sources that must be loaded and held in memory by the application are already summarized and consequently smaller in size).

4. **global.R coding**: Exactly as in step 3, it is generally possible to code an application without a `global.R` file but, as it was already explained, including this will lead to significant improvements in terms of performance in most of the cases.

5. **UI.R partial coding**: In order to understand the input/output process, `UI.R` is coded, firstly, without outputs. Splitting `UI.R` coding is clearer because it respects the information flow that was covered in *Chapter 4, Shiny Structure – Reactivity Concepts*.

6. **server.R coding**: This is the backend script.

7. **UI.R completion**: This involves the inclusion of the outputs.

8. **Styling**: This involves the final styling with CSS.

The sample application will be based on the `Adult` dataset that can be found in the UCI repository. For this particular case, it is supposed that the source data will have rows added or removed over time but the structure (that is, variable names, variable order, and so on) will remain.

Problem presentation

Let's imagine that our client or boss comes to us and says that they want us to develop an interactive web application in Shiny for `Adult` data source. They expect from us a fully functional first version and leaves, in principle, everything in our hands (including design definitions).

Once we have the dataset (or any link to it), the most sensible thing to do will be to take a look at the documentation if there is one. In this case, we have https:// archive.ics.uci.edu/ml/datasets/Adult and https://archive.ics.uci.edu/ ml/machine-learning-databases/adult/adult.names. These web pages contain summarized context information, the different variables names, and their possible values.

Although it might sound trivial, client briefs, documentations, context information, and so on are very useful pieces of information for our applications, as they will give us insights on how the source of information that we have to work on was generated and what purpose did it pursue. In this sense, it is always important to keep in mind that a successful interactive application must provide insightful information to its users and, in order to do so, the programmers need to be familiar with the database themselves.

In this case, for instance, we can see that the `fnlwgt` variable is an estimate that is calculated based on the socio-economic characteristics of the respondents. As there is no clear explanation of what this is, and we assume that the application that we are going to develop must be understood by a non-expert audience, we can take this out. The case of relationship is similar. As there is no documentation, there is no way of establishing what particular relationship this variable is describing. For this reason, we will be taking this out of the application.

Apart from reading the documentation, it is also sensible to take a look at the data sources that will be used for the application; not just know the variable names, but also take a look at the data. This can give revealing facts about, for example, which variables are important, which ones can be used as filter variables, what kind of visualizations can give insightful information, and so on.

In this case, we have to, firstly, load the data, assign the corresponding variable names, and call summaries for each variable:

```
#Retrieve Data

data.adult <- read.csv("http://archive.ics.uci.edu/ml/machine-
learning-databases/adult/adult.data", header = F)

#Assign variable names

names(data.adult) <- c("age", "workclass", "fnlwgt", "education",
"education.num", "marital.status", "occupation", "relationship",
"race", "sex", "capital.gain", "capital.loss", "hours.per.week",
"native.country","earnings")

#Apply summary for each column in data

sapply(data.adult, summary)
```

The last command will output a summary for each variable, which will correspond to its class; if it is a factor or a character, a table is returned. In the case of numeric variables, quartiles and a mean is returned.

In many cases, we can check whether any of the variables in the dataset have always the same value or a different one every time (for example, `ids`). In this particular case, for example, we can appreciate that the `age` variable has values between `17` and `90`. So, for example, if we are planning to put an age filter, it should not accept values lower than `17` or the minimum value for the variable.

For example, the `workclass` variable can give very good insights, but there is definitely some preprocessing needed as there are too many categories with an unbalanced distribution, and almost 70 percent of the sample is concentrated on the `Private` category. This can lead to misleading graphics if we want to include this variable in visualization. For example, a frequency bar chart will be dominated by the most frequent value.

Summary statistics are also not possible without preprocessing, as they will be calculated based on statistically insignificant data. In order to obtain more summarized information, some of the remaining categories can be merged with a more general one. For example, `Federal-gov`, `Local-gov`, and `State-gov` can be re-categorized into `Government`. Actually, all factor-type variables that remain in the dataset except for `earnings` and `sex` need recoding.

`native.country` seems a very interesting variable at first glance to include in the visualization. However, its multiplicity of categories in addition to its remarked concentration on United States makes it almost impossible to include it in the analysis, and also, recode the remaining categories into, for example, continents.

`capital.loss` and `capital.gain` are also variables with a very particular distribution with over 90 percent of the sample in 0. So, at first glance, we would suspect that it does not make much sense to include them in the visualization.

Finally, `education.num` and `education` are the exact same variables with the sole difference that the values in `education.num` correspond to each ordered stage in education (`1` for pre-school, `2` for 1st to 4th, and so on). This is definitely a duplication of information, but expressed differently. In some way, both express valuable information. On one hand, it is important to keep the categories in `education` because if we would like to generate a visualization with this variable, it should be definitely done with the labels and not with the numerical codes of the corresponding `education.num`.

On the other hand, `education.num` contains the order of the different stages. Consequently, the information in both variables is relevant and has to be retained. The best alternative, therefore, would be to generate a single factor variable where the numerical value and its label correspond to each other.

So far, we have made the following seven decisions:

1. Eliminate `fnlwgt` because it could be unclear to the general public.
2. Eliminate `relationship` because there is no explanation about its meaning.
3. Eliminate `native.country` due to its concentration on `United States`.
4. Eliminate `capital.loss` because of its distribution.
5. Eliminate `capital.gain` for the same reason as explained in step 2.
6. Recode all categorical variables except `sex` and `earnings` to have less but statistically more significant categories in each variable.
7. Merge `education` and `education.num` into one single variable.

Now that we have a better understanding of the data source, we will move go on to the conceptual design.

Conceptual design

Once we have a general understanding of the data involved in the application, we can decide what data is going to be in the input variables and what will be the role of each one of them. It is important to consider that input and output variables are not mutually exclusive; a variable can be used both as a part of an input and an output. Input widgets can also have different roles. They can be used as filters, aggregate variables, variables selectors for visualizations, and so on. In other words, they can be used as inputs for almost any process that can be programmed within a reactive context.

This flexibility enables us at this preprogramming stage to conceive an application with almost no restrictions. Although this is definitely an advantage, it has to be handled carefully. The need to develop an application that covers every possible aspect of the dataset, although technically possible, can produce a very confusing outcome. It is important to keep in mind that these kinds of visualizations have to communicate something to their user. So, it does not make sense to provide tons of information if it is not going to be understood.

At this stage, the developers must also work as analysts. They will need to decide what is important and what is not, find or determine what variables can be `causes`, and which ones can be `consequences`, and so on. In other words, the developer needs to generate their own hypothesis about the data source that has to be visualized.

Let's do this process in our example. Excluding the variables mentioned in the previous section, we can divide the remaining variables into three big groups: demographical, education and occupation, and earnings, which are composed as follows:

- **Demographical**: age, sex, race, and marital.status
- **Education**: education/education.num
- **Occupation and earnings**: occupation, workclass, hours.per.week, and earnings

Of course, there are probably multiple correlations between the variables of the same and different groups, but in this case, we are going to focus on the influence of the demographical variables in the rest, so we are going to generate input widgets exclusively based on demographical variables.

The outputs, however, are not going to describe only the relationship between demographical variables and the rest, but also between themselves, as this can provide insightful and easy-to-read information about demographic aspects of the data.

Following the grouping logic established previously, it would be wise to structure the application in an input area and a tab-separated output area, with one tab per group. The inputs will be on the left-hand side and the tabs on the right-hand side.

The content of each tab will depend on the level of the measurement of the variables involved. There are two numeric variables (age and hours.per.week), one ordinal (education), and the rest are categorical.

In this example, we are going to stick to traditional visualizations derived from equally traditional operations with the data available so that non-expert users can also understand it:

- **Demographics tab**: Here, four plots are displayed. The first is a simple male/female proportion bar chart, the second is also a bar chart of the race variable but controlled by gender, and the third one is a line chart of age frequency, also controlled by gender. The fourth one is a simple percentage table of the marital.status variable.

- **Education tab**: Taking advantage of its ordinal level of measurement, we can generate a descending line chart with the education categories ordered along the horizontal axis. Each point on the horizontal axis represents the number (in percentage) of people that reached that educational state. For instance, if the value in education is HS-grad, this means that the previous categories are completed as well. This graph is controlled by a categorical variable that obtains one line per category, which enables easy comparisons.

- **Occupation and earnings tab**: This contains two elements, the output of a chi-square test between earnings and any other categorical variable displayed as text, and the median of `hours per week` by `occupation` and `workclass` calculated and displayed in a table.

This will be then the application's schema:

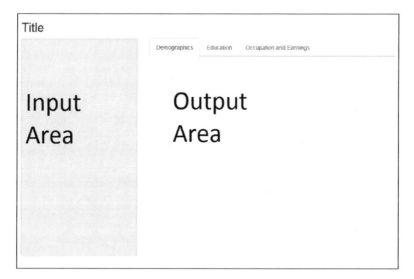

After this, we can say that our idea of how the application will be is clear, so it is time to make this real. In order to put in practice as many topics as possible covered here, this implementation will contain visualizations done with different packages, styles, and so on. Under normal circumstances, this is not recommended as it can be visually unattractive and even unclear.

However, first things first! Once we know what we are going to do, we can also arrange our data sources to make the application as optimal as possible. For this reason we should do some preprocessing on the data source prior to starting with the coding of the application.

Pre-application processing

This first coding stage must include all the processes that are completely independent from the application. Although they can be automatically scheduled eventually (for example, if the data source changes over time and has to be refreshed), we can think of processes that need to be done just once whenever the data source changes.

In our example, we will include the elimination of variables and the recoding. After this process, the processed data sources have to be saved, of course. In the following piece of code, we will load the dataset in the same way as we did before and eliminate the corresponding columns:

```
#Retrieve Data

data.adult <- read.csv("http://archive.ics.uci.edu/ml/machine-
learning-databases/adult/adult.data", header = F)

names(data.adult) <- c("age", "workclass", "fnlwgt", "education",
"education.num", "marital.status", "occupation", "relationship",
"race", "sex", "capital.gain", "capital.loss", "hours.per.week",
"native.country","earnings")

#Eliminate variables

data.adult$fnlwgt <- NULL
data.adult$relationship <- NULL
data.adult$native.country <- NULL
data.adult$capital.loss <- NULL
data.adult$capital.gain <- NULL
```

Now, it is time to the recode variables. In this case, it is a variable-by-variable customized work, as there is no way to generalize groupings between variables. The code for re-coding each one of them is explained in the next section.

Workclass

With the following line, we can obtain the proportion per category:

```
round(prop.table(table(data.adult$workclass)),4)
```

The outcome is as follows:

```
##                 ?     Federal-gov        Local-gov     Never-worked
##           0.0564          0.0295           0.0643           0.0002
##         Private    Self-emp-inc Self-emp-not-inc        State-gov
##           0.6970          0.0343           0.0780           0.0399
##      Without-pay
##           0.0004
```

As it was anticipated in the first section of this chapter, 70 percent of the sample is concentrated on `Private`. From the remaining categories, three correspond to government employments and two to self-employed ones. Both types can be merged into a single category. `Never-worked` and `Without-pay` have a very marginal contribution.

Although they probably mean different things, due to the narrow frequency of `Never-worked` and `Without-pay`, we will include them all in `Others`. The `?` category will be treated as missing. This is naturally a loss of information but reducing the dimensionality of the question, given the fact that it has narrow frequency will help the user to compare, as there will be only a few categories to see.

As there are just a few levels in this case, we can do the recoding manually. The function used for this purpose is `mapvalues()` from the `plyr` package. This receives the original labeled factor variable and two equally long vectors (`from` and `to`) that correspond to the original label and its replacement:

```
data.adult$workclass <- mapvalues(data.adult$workclass,
        from = c("Federal-gov","Local-gov", "State-gov",
        "Self-emp-inc", "Self-emp-not-inc",
        "Never-worked", "Without-pay", "?"),
        to = c(rep("Government",3), rep("Self-employed",2), rep("No-
salary",2), NA))
```

Something similar is done with the rest of the variables. The following is the recoding code for each of them:

```
#Recode marital.status

data.adult$marital.status <- mapvalues(data.adult$marital.status,
        from = c("Married-AF-spouse","Married-civ-spouse",
        "Divorced","Married-spouse-absent", "Separated"),
        to = c(rep("Married",2), rep("Divorced/Separated",3)))

#Recode occupation

data.adult$occupation <- mapvalues(data.adult$occupation, from = "?",
to = NA)

#Recode race

data.adult$race <- mapvalues(data.adult$race, from = "Amer-Indian-
Eskimo", to = "Other")
```

After this, `education` and `education.num` are merged with `education`, and `education.num` is erased:

```
unique.education <- unique(data.adult[,c("education.
num","education")])
levels.ordered <- as.character(unique.education$education[order(uniqu
e.education$education.num)])

data.adult$education <- as.factor(data.adult$education.num)

levels(data.adult$education) <- levels.ordered

data.adult$education.num <- NULL
```

Finally, the dataset is saved in a binary file (ideally, `.rda` or `.rds`), due to performance and space:

```
save(data.adult, file = "Path_to_application/rawdata_adult.rda")
```

This will be the complete script:

```
library(plyr)

#Retrieve Data

data.adult <- read.csv("http://archive.ics.uci.edu/ml/machine-
learning-databases/adult/adult.data", header = F, strip.white = T)

names(data.adult) <- c("age", "workclass", "fnlwgt", "education",
"education.num", "marital.status", "occupation", "relationship",
"race", "sex", "capital.gain", "capital.loss", "hours.per.week",
"native.country","earnings")

data.adult$fnlwgt <- NULL
data.adult$relationship <- NULL
data.adult$native.country <- NULL
data.adult$capital.loss <- NULL
data.adult$capital.gain <- NULL

#Recode workclass

data.adult$workclass <- mapvalues(data.adult$workclass,
                               from = c("Federal-gov","Local-gov",
"State-gov",
                                       "Self-emp-inc", "Self-emp-
not-inc",
                                       "Never-worked", "Without-
```

```
pay", "?"),
                                         to = c(rep("Government",3),
rep("Self-employed",2), rep("Others",2), NA))


#Recode marital.statuss

data.adult$marital.status <- mapvalues(data.adult$marital.status,
                                 from = c("Married-AF-
spouse","Married-civ-spouse",
                                         "Divorced","Married-spouse-
absent", "Separated"),
                                 to = c(rep("Married",2),
rep("Divorced/Separated",3)))

#Recode occupation

data.adult$occupation <- mapvalues(data.adult$occupation, from = "?",
to = NA)

#Recode race

data.adult$race <- mapvalues(data.adult$race, from = "Amer-Indian-
Eskimo", to = "Other")

#Merge education and education.num

unique.education <- unique(data.adult[,c("education.
num","education")])
levels.ordered <- as.character(unique.education$education[order(uniqu
e.education$education.num)])

data.adult$education <- as.factor(data.adult$education.num)

levels(data.adult$education) <- levels.ordered

data.adult$eduaction.num <- NULL

#Save data

save(data.adult, file = "Path_to_application/rawdata_adult.rda")
```

global.R coding

While the previous section covered processes that had to be done only once whenever the data source changes, `global.R` will include all the actions that can be done just once per session, for example, see the following:

- Data source loading
- Library calls
- Custom functions sourcing

In our case, apart from loading the dataset and calling the corresponding libraries, we will need to generate a vector that contains the names of all the categorical variables. This will be used in one of the variables selectors. Of course, this last step can be avoided and the list of variables can be hardcoded.

However, in terms of the application's maintenance, it is much wiser to do it this way because if the data source changes (for example, a new categorical variable is added) and we want to include this in the same way as the others, we should be constantly updating this list manually. Although this might be trivial in this example, it can be very necessary in others, especially when the data source's structure changes constantly.

global.R

`earnings` is excluded from the vector because it is the variable that has to be crossed against in the chi-square test:

```
library(shiny)
library(googleVis)
library(reshape2)
library(ggplot2)

load("rawdata_adult.rda")

factor.vars <- names(which(sapply(data.adult, class) == "factor"))
factor.vars <- setdiff(factor.vars,"earnings")
```

UI.R partial coding

As it was said before, the input widgets are the first part of the application that must be coded. In this case, almost all the widgets are on the side panel except the selectors that are used in the education-descending line chart and the earnings chi-square test that are in their corresponding tabs. Also, it is recommended to generate the application's frontend structure at this stage. So, the `UI.R` code that we have so far would be as shown in the following section.

UI.R

As it may be noted, the arguments of the widgets builders are determined dynamically. The reason behind this is exactly the same as in the creation of `factor.vars` in `global.R`: avoid hardcoding. Of course, there are some cases (for example, the sex variable) where this will be unnecessary, as it is impossible that the categories were changed even with a change in the data source. However, in cases such as age, it is perfectly possible that the minimum and maximum values change. So, this dynamic referencing guarantees that the input's limits are the same as the dataset's:

```
library(shiny)

# Starting line
shinyUI(fluidPage(

  # Application title
  titlePanel("Adult Dataset"),

  sidebarLayout(

    sidebarPanel(
      h1("Gender"),
      checkboxGroupInput("gender", "Choose the genders",
                         choices = levels(data.adult$sex),
                         selected = levels(data.adult$sex)),
      h1("Age"),
      sliderInput("minage", "Select lower limit", min(data.adult$age),
max(data.adult$age), value = min(data.adult$age), step = 1),
      sliderInput("maxage", "Select upper limit", min(data.adult$age),
max(data.adult$age), value = max(data.adult$age), step = 1),

      h1("Ethnic group"),
      selectInput("ethnic", "Select ethnic groups", choices =
levels(data.adult$race),
                  selected = levels(data.adult$race), multiple = T),
      h1("Marital Status"),
      selectInput("marital.stat", "Select marital status", choices =
levels(data.adult$marital.status),
                  selected = levels(data.adult$marital.status),
multiple = T),

      actionButton("submitter","Submit")
    ),
```

```
    mainPanel(
      tabsetPanel(
       tabPanel("Demographics",
             column(6,div("Gender Distribution (in %)", class =
"title"),
                      div("Age Distribution (in %) by Gender", class
= "title")),
             column(6,div("Ethnicity distribution by gender (in
%)", class = "title"),
                      div("Marital Status distribution (in %)", class
= "title"))),
             tabPanel("Education",
                    div("Educational Curve", class = "title"),
                    selectInput("edvar","Choose the variable to
compare",
                            choices = c("sex","race",
"marital.status"),
                            selected = "sex")),
             tabPanel("Occupation and Earnings",
                    div("Earning Chi test", class = "title"),
                    selectInput("earnvar","Choose the variable to
run the test with",
                            choices = factor.vars, selected =
factor.vars[1]),
                    div("Activity summary", class = "title"))
        )
      )
     )
  ))
```

There is only one input where its options are hardcoded: that is, edvar. This is because the election of the variables is firstly totally arbitrary (and for this reason, they should be hardcoded somewhere), and secondly because they are not used anywhere else. If the same options were used in another part of the application, it would have been better to store them in a separate object that is coded on global.R.

server.R coding

After analysis and the application's design, this is definitely the most important stage of coding. A well-programmed backend is the key to performance and consequently effective visualizations. In this part, as in every backend process, the focus should be on producing the output with as little code and processing as possible. In order to achieve this, the key is to avoid repetition.

In our example, all the outputs are produced from the same dataset, which is basically the data source filtered by the corresponding input values. As it was explained in *Chapter 5, Shiny in Depth – A Deep Dive into Shiny's World*, there is no need to generate the same object for every visualization, as a reactive object can be used instead. In this example, a reactive object is precisely used:

```
#Reactive subset

data.sset <- reactive({
  input$submitter
  isolate({
    subset(data.adult, sex %in% input$gender & age >= input$minage &
    age <= input$maxage & marital.status %in% input$marital.stat &
    race %in% input$ethnic)

  })

})
```

This piece of code generates the `data.sset` reactive object, which will be used by all the outputs. Notice that the code for the generation of this object is enclosed inside an `isolate()` clause. This piece of script is triggered once the button is hit, which means that the dataset is not updated until then. With this object, the different plots are generated as explained in the following sections.

Gender bar chart

For this visualization, an extra reactive object is needed in order to determine which colors specified under `col` will be used. This is necessary because otherwise, the color vector will be updated but the dataset will not, and the outcome would be two bars of the same color:

```
genders.amount <- reactive({
  input$submitter
  isolate({length(input$gender)})
})

output$genderbars <- renderPlot({

  barplot(prop.table(table(data.sset()$sex)) * 100,
  col = c("red","blue")[1:genders.amount()],
  ylab = "Proportion (in %)")

})
```

The function used to generate this plot is `barplot()` from the base graphics. `barplot()` takes the named vector argument and uses the values to determine the height and the names to label the columns.

Age chart

The age chart is done with `ggplot2`. In order to draw two series, `ggplot2` expects that one of the variables of the data argument is the grouping variable. For this reason, a table of `sex` and `age` was generated and melted. The melting turned the 2 x 73 matrix (2 values for `sex`, 73 for `age`) into a 146 x 3 data frame (one row per age-sex combination and its frequency):

```
output$agechart <- renderPlot({

  agg.set <- with(data.sset(), melt(prop.table(table(sex,age),1)))
  agg.set$value <- agg.set$value *  100
  age_sex.plot <- ggplot(agg.set, aes(x=age,y=value,group=sex, colour
= sex))
  age_sex.plot <- age_sex.plot + geom_line()
  age_sex.plot <- age_sex.plot + theme(legend.title=element_blank())
  age_sex.plot <- age_sex.plot + labs(y = "Proportion (in %)")
  age_sex.plot <- age_sex.plot + labs(x = "Age")
  return(age_sex.plot)
})
```

As all the necessary information was passed in the `ggplot` object creation (the data and the `aes`), the plotting layer (`geom_line()`) was added without any arguments. The successive layers were used to customize legends and actually override the already existing ones.

Ethnic bar chart

The first part is similar to the following one. However, as the function `googleVis` function expects the data to be ordered differently, it was necessary to rearrange the data in an `nx2` data frame, where the columns represent the porcentual frequency of females and males respectively:

```
output$ethnicbars <- renderGvis({

  agg.set <- with(data.sset(), melt(prop.table(table(race,sex),1)))
  agg.set$value <- agg.set$value *  100
  agg.set <- dcast(agg.set,formula = race ~ sex, value.var = "value")
  ret <- gvisColumnChart(agg.set, xvar = "race", yvar =
c("Female","Male"),
  options=list( height="300px"))

})
```

Under `yvar`, `gvisColumnChart()` expects a vector with the column names that contain the numeric values that will be represented in the bars plotted, either one next to the other or stacked.

Marital status

This piece of code is definitely very easy to understand. A table is created, converted to a data frame, values are turned to percentages, and returned:

```
output$marital.statustable <- renderTable({

  marital.status.table <- as.data.frame.table(prop.table(table(data.
sset()$marital.status)))
  marital.status.table[,2] <- round(marital.status.table[,2] * 100)
  names(marital.status.table) <- c("Marital.Status","Percentage")

  return(marital.status.table)

})
```

Education curve

As it was explained before, this visualization relies on a cumulative logic in its classification; the value in these variables is the maximum level achieved, which means that the person has completed the stages that come before this. Also, in this case there is a second challenge; the control variable was determined by the `edvar` input widget:

```
output$educationcurve <- renderGvis({

  freq.table <- with(data.sset(), prop.table(table(mget(c(input$edvar,
"education")))))
  cum.perc <- apply(freq.table,1,function(x) cumsum(rev(x))/sum(x))
  cum.perc <- cum.perc[nrow(cum.perc):1,]
  cum.perc <- as.data.frame(cum.perc)
  cum.perc <- cbind(education = row.names(cum.perc),cum.perc)
  ret <- gvisLineChart(cum.perc, xvar = "education",yvar = names(cum.
perc)[-1],
  options = list(hAxis = "{textStyle: {fontSize : '6px'}}",
  vAxis = "{format : 'percent'}",
  height = "400px"))
  return(ret)
})
```

The first table has to be between the `education` variable and the input variable. For this reason, `mget()` along with `with()` is used. `with()` treats the passed dataset as an environment, and `mget()` returns the values of the objects based on the name reference under the environment it is called. These names are passed as a character vector. This `table()` call produces an `nxm` matrix, where `n` is the number of the categories of the input variable and `m` is the number of the categories of `education`.

Then, `cumsum()` is applied to every row, but in an inverted order (`rev()`). `cumsum()` performs a cumulative sum, and as the original table generated previously contains the education values in ascending order (preschool first, doctorate last), we need to do the cumulative sum in the inverse order to get the number of people who reached (and completed) that educational stage. However, this process will output the table in the inverse order. For this reason, the object is indexed inversely from its last value to its first one (`nrow(cum.perc):1`).

The object is then casted in a data frame (`googleVis` only accepts data frames) and their row names are created as a column. If this is not done, the object cannot be passed to `gvisLineChart`. Finally, the plotting function is called. As in bar chart in `gvis`, the `yvar` argument can take multiple variables. However, as we don't know the names of the plotting variables because they will depend on the input variable passed, `yvar` is defined for all the names of `cum.perc` except the first one, which is education.

Earnings chi-square test

The created table is used to perform a chi-squared test. From this test, p-value and chi-square value are used to generate a text in HTML:

```
output$earningsplot <- renderUI({

   freq.table <- with(data.sset(), table(mget(c(input$earnvar,"earnin
gs"))))
   chi.test <- chisq.test(freq.table)

   html.text <- paste0("p value: ",round(chi.test$p.value,5),"<br><br>
chi squared statistic: ",round(chi.test$statistic))

   return(HTML(html.text))

})
```

 A chi-square test is a statistical test that proves whether there is an association between two categorical variables.

It is important to take into account that when passing HTML, the output is passed through HTML() before returning it. Although renderUI is used to specifically generate reactive user inputs (user inputs whose values depend on reactive values), it is basically an HTML wrapper, that is, it can contain any HTML element.

Activity summary

aggregate() generates a data frame with the combination of each occupation and workclass categories and its corresponding median of the hours.per.week variable. This output does not really reveal meaningful insights, but it is a good excuse to show how JavaScript's data table output works:

```
output$activity.summary <- renderDataTable({

  aggregate(hours.per.week ~ occupation + workclass, data = data.
sset(),FUN = "median")

}, options = list(pageLength = 10, columnDefs = "{width : '20%'}"))
```

These pieces of code conform to the complete server.R script as follows:

```
library(shiny)

#initialization of server.R
shinyServer(function(input, output) {

  #Reactive subset

  data.sset <- reactive({
  input$submitter
      isolate({
      subset(data.adult, sex %in% input$gender & age >= input$minage &
              age <= input$maxage & marital.status %in% input$marital.
stat &
              race %in% input$ethnic)

  })

  })


  #### Demograhpics chart ####

  genders.amount <- reactive({
    input$submitter
```

```
        isolate({length(input$gender)})
    })

    output$genderbars <- renderPlot({

        barplot(prop.table(table(data.sset()$sex)) * 100,
                col = c("red","blue")[1:genders.amount()],
                ylab = "Proportion (in %)")

    })



    output$agechart <- renderPlot({

        agg.set <- with(data.sset(), melt(prop.table(table(sex,age),1)))
        agg.set$value <- agg.set$value *  100
        age_sex.plot <- ggplot(agg.set, aes(x=age,y=value,group=sex, colour
    = sex))
        age_sex.plot <- age_sex.plot + geom_line()
        age_sex.plot <- age_sex.plot + theme(legend.title=element_blank())
        age_sex.plot <- age_sex.plot + labs(y = "Proportion (in %)")
        age_sex.plot <- age_sex.plot + labs(x = "Age")
        return(age_sex.plot)
    })



    output$ethnicbars <- renderGvis({

        agg.set <- with(data.sset(), melt(prop.table(table(race,sex),1)))
        agg.set$value <- agg.set$value *  100
        agg.set <- dcast(agg.set,formula = race ~ sex, value.var = "value")
        ret <- gvisColumnChart(agg.set, xvar = "race", yvar =
    c("Female","Male"),
            options=list( height="300px"))

    })

    output$marital.statustable <- renderTable({

        marital.status.table <- as.data.frame.table(prop.table(table(data.
    sset()$marital.status)))
        marital.status.table[,2] <- round(marital.status.table[,2] * 100)
        names(marital.status.table) <- c("Marital.Status","Percentage")
```

```
      return(marital.status.table)


  })


  #### Education curve ####


  output$educationcurve <- renderGvis({


      freq.table <- with(data.sset(), prop.
table(table(mget(c(input$edvar, "education")))))
      cum.perc <- apply(freq.table,1,function(x) cumsum(rev(x))/sum(x))
      cum.perc <- cum.perc[nrow(cum.perc):1,]
      cum.perc <- as.data.frame(cum.perc)
      cum.perc <- cbind(education = row.names(cum.perc),cum.perc)
      ret <- gvisLineChart(cum.perc, xvar = "education",yvar = names(cum.
perc)[-1],
         options = list(hAxis = "{textStyle: {fontSize : '6px'}}",
         vAxis = "{format : 'percent'}",
         height = "400px"))
      return(ret)
  })



  #### Occupation and earnings ####


  output$earningsplot <- renderUI({


      freq.table <- with(data.sset(), table(mget(c(input$earnvar,"earnin
gs"))))
      chi.test <- chisq.test(freq.table)


      html.text <- paste0("p value: ",round(chi.test$p.value,5),"<br><br>
chi squared statistic: ",round(chi.test$statistic))


      return(HTML(html.text))


  })


  output$activity.summary <- renderDataTable({


      aggregate(hours.per.week ~ occupation + workclass, data = data.
sset(),FUN = "median")


  }, options = list(pageLength = 10, columnDefs = "{width : '20%'}"))



  })
```

UI.R completion

The only thing remaining to do in order to have a fully functional application is display the outputs in UI.R. As it was explained before, each render variable has a corresponding output counterpart. Back to our example, as explained in the following sections this is how UI.R is completed.

UI.R

As it has been explained, every output name corresponds to an object in the output list created in server.R:

```
library(shiny)

# Starting line
shinyUI(fluidPage(

  # Application title
  titlePanel("Adult Dataset"),

  sidebarLayout(

    # Sidebar

    sidebarPanel(
      h1("Gender"),
      checkboxGroupInput("gender", "Choose the genders",
      choices = levels(data.adult$sex),
      selected = levels(data.adult$sex)),
      h1("Age"),
      sliderInput("minage", "Select lower limit", min(data.adult$age),
max(data.adult$age), value = min(data.adult$age), step = 1),
      sliderInput("maxage", "Select upper limit", min(data.adult$age),
max(data.adult$age), value = max(data.adult$age), step = 1),

      h1("Ethnic group"),
      selectInput("ethnic", "Select ethnic groups", choices =
levels(data.adult$race),
      selected = levels(data.adult$race), multiple = T),
      h1("Marital Status"),
      selectInput("marital.stat", "Select marital status", choices =
levels(data.adult$marital.status),
      selected = levels(data.adult$marital.status), multiple = T),

      actionButton("submitter","Submit")
```

```
    ),


  #Main Panel
    mainPanel(
      tabsetPanel(
        tabPanel("Demographics",
        column(6,div("Gender Distribution (in %)", class = "title"),
        br(),
        plotOutput("genderbars", height = "300px", width = "80%"),
        div("Age Distribution (in %) by Gender", class = "title"),
        br(),
        plotOutput("agechart", height = "300px", width = "80%")),
        column(6,div("Ethnicity distribution by gender (in %)", class =
"title"),
        br(),
        htmlOutput("ethnicbars"),
        div("Marital Status distribution (in %)", class = "title"),
        br(),br(),
        tableOutput("marital.statustable"))
        ),
        tabPanel("Education",
        div("Educational Curve", class = "title"),
        selectInput("edvar","Choose the variable to compare",choices =
c("sex","race", "marital.status"), selected = "sex"),
        htmlOutput("educationcurve")),
        tabPanel("Occupation and Earnings",
        div("Earning Chi test", class = "title"),
        selectInput("earnvar","Choose the variable to run the test
with",
        choices = factor.vars, selected = factor.vars[1]),
        htmlOutput("earningsplot"),
        br(),br(),
        div("Activity summary", class = "title"),
        dataTableOutput("activity.summary")
        )
        )
      )
    )
))
```

In the first tab, the outputs are enclosed in a `column()` tag in order to line them up and have two columns. Additionally, it will be necessary that every visualization has the same size. For this reason, width and height were specified, as plot outputs cannot receive a class argument and cannot be handled by CSS.

Styling

Once we have a complete working application, it is time for some styling with CSS. In the following example, just some fonts are changed. It is always good, when possible, to control the styles with CSS. There are some widgets, such as plot outputs that are not so easy to handle as the tags assignment is restricted.

In the following CSS, saved as `style.css`, some of the texts are styled as follows:

```
.title {
  font-size: 18px;
  font-weight: bold;
}
h1 {
  font-style: italic;
  font-family: impact;
}
```

As it was explained in *Chapter 8, Shiny and HTML/JavaScript*, CSS stylesheets can be included with an `includeCSS()` statement inside `UI.R`:

```
# Starting line
shinyUI(fluidPage(

  #CSS styling
  includeCSS("PATH_to_CSS_file/style.css"),
  # Application title
  titlePanel("Adult Dataset"),
```

Discovering insights in the application

With an application ready to use, it is always rewarding to find out that it fulfills its purpose. In this case, it would be to discover insights visually from the data.

The following screenshot is very illustrative about the educational possibilities in the past. As it may be noted, the **Male** and **Female** lines are very similar until HS-grad. In fact, the percentage of females that reached this educational state is slightly higher. But after this, the trend is drastically reverse, and it is the **Male** line that is clearly above the **Female** one. Although further research should be done in order to figure out the causes of this phenomenon (the reader can make their own hypothesis), it is clear that the possibilities of studying were not the same ones:

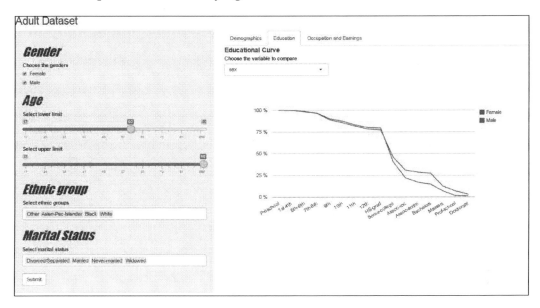

The age distribution by gender presents curious results as well. It seems that, at least in the sample collected in this dataset, the distribution by ages is not similar; women's curve has a peak between 18 to 25, while men have are concentrated on the 30 to 45 segment approximately:

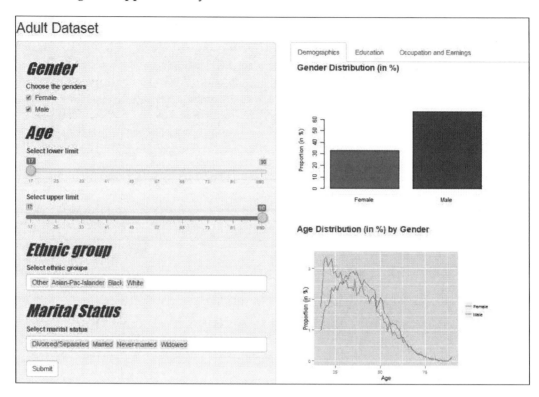

These are only some examples of what a web application with suitable data visualizations can tell us from the data source that we are analyzing. In this sense, Shiny and R are great allies because they can take the integration of data analysis and data presentation to a whole new level; an almost limitless backend built on one of the most important programming languages in data science with an entire intuitive, user-friendly and extensible framework. In summary, anything that can be programmed can be coded in R and everything that can be displayed in a web browser can be produced in Shiny.

Shiny is not just another way of creating web applications, but it is also an open source-based key with practically no restrictions when it comes to communicating things with data.

Summary

This chapter closes this introductory book to Shiny. Not only did it explain how to code an application from scratch, but also showed what the entire process is about. It does not make much sense to possess perfect programming skills when it comes to these kinds of applications and have no idea about the need that that the application is supposed to fulfill.

This chapter is conceived in the same way as the whole book is. It is not just coding that makes a good application developer, but it is also about thinking of the problem as a whole and consequently of the application as a tool for users with no technical knowledge (that is, the vast majority of the users) to unveil insights about the data they are analyzing. In the end, data visualization is just communication.

Reference

Lichman, M. (2013). UCI Machine Learning Repository (http://archive.ics.uci.edu/ml). Irvine, CA: University of California, School of Information and Computer Science.

Index

Thank you for buying
Learning Shiny

About Packt Publishing

Packt, pronounced 'packed', published its first book, *Mastering phpMyAdmin for Effective MySQL Management*, in April 2004, and subsequently continued to specialize in publishing highly focused books on specific technologies and solutions.

Our books and publications share the experiences of your fellow IT professionals in adapting and customizing today's systems, applications, and frameworks. Our solution-based books give you the knowledge and power to customize the software and technologies you're using to get the job done. Packt books are more specific and less general than the IT books you have seen in the past. Our unique business model allows us to bring you more focused information, giving you more of what you need to know, and less of what you don't.

Packt is a modern yet unique publishing company that focuses on producing quality, cutting-edge books for communities of developers, administrators, and newbies alike. For more information, please visit our website at www.packtpub.com.

About Packt Open Source

In 2010, Packt launched two new brands, Packt Open Source and Packt Enterprise, in order to continue its focus on specialization. This book is part of the Packt Open Source brand, home to books published on software built around open source licenses, and offering information to anybody from advanced developers to budding web designers. The Open Source brand also runs Packt's Open Source Royalty Scheme, by which Packt gives a royalty to each open source project about whose software a book is sold.

Writing for Packt

We welcome all inquiries from people who are interested in authoring. Book proposals should be sent to author@packtpub.com. If your book idea is still at an early stage and you would like to discuss it first before writing a formal book proposal, then please contact us; one of our commissioning editors will get in touch with you.

We're not just looking for published authors; if you have strong technical skills but no writing experience, our experienced editors can help you develop a writing career, or simply get some additional reward for your expertise.

Building Interactive Graphs with
Graphs with
ggplot2 and Shiny
Christophe Ladroue

Building Interactive Graphs with ggplot2 and Shiny [Video]

ISBN: 978-1-78328-433-7   Duration: 01:51 hours

Build stunning graphics and interactive visuals for real-time data analysis and visualization with ggplot2 and Shiny

1. Generate complex interactive web pages using R and produce publication-ready graphics in a principled manner.

2. Use aesthetics effectively to map your data into graphical elements.

3. Customize your graphs according to your specific needs without wasting time on programming issues.

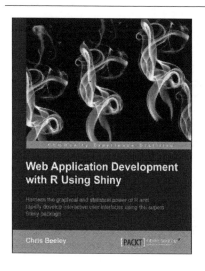

Web Application Development
with R Using Shiny

Chris Beeley

Web Application Development with R Using Shiny

ISBN: 978-1-78328-447-4   Paperback: 110 pages

Harness the graphical and statistical power of R and rapidly develop interactive user interfaces using the superb Shiny package

1. Helps you to use Shiny's built in functions to produce engaging and useful user interfaces in hours, not days.

2. Enables you to extend Shiny using JavaScript and jQuery with minimal coding.

3. Shows you how to write cutting-edge interactive content for the Web.

Please check **www.PacktPub.com** for information on our titles

R Machine Learning Essentials

ISBN: 978-1-78398-774-0   Paperback: 218 pages

Gain quick access to the machine learning concepts and practical applications using the R development environment

1. Build machine learning algorithms using the most powerful tools in R.

2. Identify business problems and solve them by developing effective solutions.

3. Hands-on tutorial explaining the concepts through lots of practical examples, tips and tricks.

Machine Learning with R

ISBN: 978-1-78216-214-8   Paperback: 396 pages

Learn how to use R to apply powerful machine learning methods and gain an insight into real-world applications

1. Harness the power of R for statistical computing and data science.

2. Use R to apply common machine learning algorithms with real-world applications.

3. Prepare, examine, and visualize data for analysis.

4. Understand how to choose between machine learning models.

Please check **www.PacktPub.com** for information on our titles

Made in the USA
Lexington, KY
27 June 2018